THE WORK OF MERCY

THE
WORK
OF
MERCY

Being the Hands and Heart of Christ

MARK P. SHEA

SERVANT
BOOKS

PUBLISHED BY ST. ANTHONY MESSENGER PRESS
CINCINNATI, OHIO

Unless otherwise noted, Scripture passages have been taken from the *Revised Standard Version*, Catholic edition. Copyright 1946, 1952, 1971 by the Division of Christian Education of the National Council of Churches of Christ in the USA. Used by permission. All rights reserved.

Scripture passages marked *KJV* have been taken from the *King James Bible*.

Cover and book design by Mark Sullivan
Cover image © istockphoto.com | james steidl

LIBRARY OF CONGRESS CATALOGING-IN-PUBLICATION DATA
Shea, Mark P.
The work of mercy : being the hands and heart of Christ / Mark P. Shea.
p. cm.
Includes bibliographical references (p.   ) and index.
ISBN 978-1-61636-009-2 (pbk. : alk. paper) 1. Corporal works of mercy. 2. Spiritual works of mercy. I. Title.
BV4647.M4S54 2011
241'.4—dc23
2011037303

ISBN 978-1-61636-009-2

Published by Servant Books, an imprint of St. Anthony Messenger Press.
28 W. Liberty St.
Cincinnati, OH 45202
www.AmericanCatholic.org
www.ServantBooks.org

Printed in the United States of America

Printed on acid-free paper

11 12 13 14 15   5 4 3 2 1

To my beloved Janet,
who has been a sacrament of mercy
to countless people,
including me.

CONTENTS

FOREWORD

*A*T THE VERY HEART OF the gospel are the corporal and spiritual works of mercy. Just as Jesus was God "hidden" in the flesh, mercy is the incarnational echo of God's presence in our world. His light shines forth through you and me, powerfully illuminating the dark places and guiding us along the path of sanctification.

During the years of my spiritual pilgrimage toward the Roman Church, I encountered the radical mission of Mother Teresa, a powerful paradigm of God's mercy: faith in action. I was inspired to embrace, however imperfectly, a life of service, which ultimately led to the founding of Mercy Corps. We are all called—even commanded—to live as incarnational witnesses in a world crying out for the compassionate touch of Christ. If crisis equals opportunity, we have a veritable banquet of possibilities before us to engage!

When I learned that my friend Mark Shea was writing this book, I knew his incredible Chestertonian wit and words of wisdom would penetrate the pages with conviction and motivation to walk a path, drawing his readers closer to God and to "the least of these." In the end, we actually become the beneficiaries of our growing commitment to pray and obey by practicing "true religion" (see James 1:27).

Together, we can work to make the world a better place while reaping the benefits of transformation, both within and "out there."

Dan O'Neill, founder of Mercy Corps

www.mercycorps.org

Thanks above all to God, the Father, Son, and Holy Spirit, from whom, with whom, and through whom this book and all things exist. Blessed be he!

The Fam: I'm glad you are, and I thank God for you all!

Brian Saint-Paul, who liked this stuff first.

Cynthia Cavnar: For believing in this book.

Dan O'Neill, who has done more of the works of mercy than anyone I know, and whose experience as the head of Mercy Corps was an invaluable help in writing this book.

My dear friend Sherry Weddell and the gang at the Catherine of Siena Institute in Colorado Springs: You guys do awesome work!

The Curps, dear friends in the communion of saints.

G.K. Chesterton, one of my heroes.

C.S. Lewis, yet another of my heroes.

The kind readers of *Inside Catholic* and *Crisis*, upon whom I experimentally air my ideas.

The people of Blessed Sacrament parish in Seattle: Thanks for being our home till we reach our Long Home.

Also special thanks to Sts. Jerome, Athanasius, Anthony of the Desert, Francis de Sales, Dominic, Tertius, and, of course, Mama Mary, on whose constant intercession I rely for help. *Ora pro nobis.*

Introduction to the
Corporal and Spiritual Works of Mercy

*J*ESUS TOLD THE PARABLE OF the sheep and the goats. This does not
seem like a news flash until we turn away from observing the obvious
and begin to talk about soteriology, a three-dollar word for that
branch of Christian theology concerned with the question "What
must we do to be saved?"

For early Christians the answer was brief: "Believe in the Lord
Jesus Christ!"—words compact with deeply incarnational meaning.
If you believed in Jesus, it was taken for granted that you didn't
simply hold a theory about him; you were called to be his disciple and
reorder your entire life in conformity with his will. So Paul habitu-
ally spoke of the "obedience of faith" (Romans 1:5), and James likewise said that "faith without works is dead" (James 2:20, *KJV*).

This commonsense understanding of faith continued to reign for
a millennium and a half. But enthusiasts in the sixteenth century
came up with a definition of faith that lost contact with the
Incarnation. This definition basically said that "faith alone" saved and
that, consequently, it didn't really matter what you did, just so long as

you believed that Jesus would forgive you for doing it. Luther, for instance, famously said: "Be a sinner and sin boldly, but believe and rejoice in Christ even more boldly for he is victorious over sin, death, and the world. As long as we are here in this world we have to sin. This life is not a dwelling place of righteousness." He topped it with "No sin will separate us from the Lamb, even though we commit fornication and murder a thousand times a day."[1]

You can sort of see what he's getting at. Yes, Jesus does say, "Forgive seventy times seven" (see Matthew 18:22) and binds himself implicitly to the promise that he will do as much if we are truly repentant. Yes, the sacraments of baptism and reconciliation can and have forgiven stupendous crimes. (Reflect on the fact that Hans Frank, Gauleiter of Poland and the murderer of roughly four million men, women, and children, sought the sacrament of reconciliation before he was hanged and was reconciled with Christ and the Church.)

But that doesn't mean "Murder four million more and you'll still be all right." Luther's rhetorical flourish may have felt good, but "sin boldly" is counsel rejected by Luther's hero, Paul, who declared:

> What shall we say then? Are we to continue in sin that grace may abound? By no means! How can we who died to sin still live in it? (Romans 6:1–2)

It is not, however, counsel that was rejected by a great deal of Protestantism in Luther's train.

To be sure, most Evangelicals holding a "Once Saved, Always Saved" (OSAS) theology would not say, "Sin boldly!" Rather, they say that there will be unspecified bad consequences for the Christian who sins gravely. But the pernicious notion that salvation and deeds have no essential connection remains. So, while Evangelical Christian culture warriors might be willing to say that *non*-Christians face damnation, they often insist that Christians still have "assurance of salvation" since they "accepted Jesus into their heart as their personal Lord and Savior." Fail to perform that verbal ritual and (according to OSAS theory) our righteous deeds are like filthy rags in God's sight (see Isaiah 64:6). Perform that ritual and nothing can keep you out of heaven (according to OSAS theory).

Because of this theory, many Evangelical Protestants think Catholics are all about "salvation by works," and many Catholics, to whom this talk about "accepting Jesus" is foreign lingo, often fan the flames of Evangelical fear by saying, "But I go to Mass!" or "I help out at the soup kitchen," or some other variation on what Evangelicals tend to see as "works righteousness." So the conversation devolves into two monologues in two different Christian dialects as the Evangelical sits in judgment of the hell-bound Catholic and the Catholic becomes increasingly mystified by the Evangelical jargon.

My approach to Evangelicals who ask "If you died tonight, why would God let you into heaven?" is a bit different. I don't point to the good-works thing; I just tell them that I'd be happy to ask Jesus into my heart as my personal Lord and Savior (again). Then I tell my Evangelical friend I will go to Mass and say a word of thanks to Mary for this happy conversation.

Bam! Suddenly it's not "once saved, always saved" after all. Rather, I must do a good work pronto. Namely, I have to stop going to Mass, and I especially have to stop talking to and about Mary. In fact, I am often informed that I don't really have faith at all because of my Bad Work of belonging to the wrong church.

The beautiful irony of all this is that it shows that "salvation by faith alone" is not believed even by its adherents. Instead, it makes plain that if you really believe something, that belief *must* be expressed in actions or it's just a fantasy or a theory. In this case, the good work I must do is "renounce the Catholic Church." That particular course of proposed faith in action is, of course, all wet. But the idea of faith in action is itself sound as a bell.

Jesus was the first person in our tradition to point that out, which is why neither he nor his apostles ever talked about salvation through "faith alone"—except James, who condemned the idea as preposterous (see James 2:24). Instead, Jesus spoke of *salvation* in precisely the way that his disciple John spoke of *him*: as Word made flesh. When Zacchaeus pledged to pay back fourfold all he had stolen, Jesus did not rebuke him for trying to buy salvation with his filthy works of righteousness. He commended him as a true son of Abraham and told him that salvation had come to his house (see Luke 19:1–10). And when Christ in Matthew 25 talked about the salvation of the nations, he didn't theorize about faith alone but instead talked about what Catholic tradition would later call the corporal works of mercy:

> Then the king will say to those at his right hand, "Come, O blessed of my Father, inherit the kingdom prepared for you from the foundation of the world; for I was hungry and you gave me food, I was thirsty and you gave me drink, I was a stranger and you welcomed me, I was naked and you clothed

me, I was sick and you visited me, I was in prison and you
came to me." (Matthew 25:34–36)

This is not amenable to neat Evangelical categories of "saved" and
"lost." The saved sheep had no idea it was Christ they were serving.
They never so much as heard of Jesus, much less asked him into their
hearts as their personal Lord and Savior. Nor (with all due respect to
the theory of Feeneyite enthusiasts that only members of the visible
Catholic Church are saved) did the saved sheep indicate the slightest
familiarity with baptism or the sacraments. They were members of
"the nations" (that is, gentiles, goyim, outsiders). Their baffled reply
was "Lord, when did we see you hungry? thirsty?" and so on. They
had no idea it was Jesus they were serving in the poor, dispossessed,
naked, and wretched. They just thought they were doing the decent
thing. And yet, to them, the king spoke a word of neither rebuke nor
reproach for their "works salvation" nor a syllable about their righteous works being like filthy rags, nor a peep about their failure to ask
Jesus into their hearts as Savior. He said nothing about their lack of
the sacraments. None of this was according to the standard
Evangelical (or Feeneyite) playbook.

Likewise, the goats heard none of the words an Evangelical or
Feeneyite would expect about failure to make a good profession of
faith in the Trinity or the saving work of Christ on the cross. There
was nothing about a personal decision for Jesus or any sacrament. In
the parable, what was make-or-break for the goats as well as the
sheep was how they treated the "least of these."

Now, as Catholics, we must note that the parable of the sheep and
the goats is not the only thing Jesus has to say about salvation. So we

mustn't pretend the parable is fatal to the sacramental vision. He who gives us the parable also tells us, "Unless one is born of water and the Spirit, he cannot enter the kingdom of God" (John 3:5), and, "Unless you eat the flesh of the Son of man and drink his blood, you have no life in you" (John 6:53). But then the Feeneyite must also remember that this is the same Jesus who tells the unbaptized and Eucharist-deprived good thief, "Truly, I say to you, today you will be with me in Paradise" (Luke 23:43). Clearly, we are dealing with a Savior who doesn't fit into our little systems of order. What gives?

The key is the simple recollection of St. John of the Cross: "At the evening of life, we shall be judged on our love."[2]

The point of the parable of the sheep and the goats is not "You don't need faith in Jesus in order to be saved." Nor is it "Everybody cut off from the sacraments is most assuredly doomed." The point is that, in Gerard Manley Hopkins's words:

> Christ plays in ten thousand places,
> Lovely in limbs, and lovely in eyes not his
> To the Father through the features of men's faces.[3]

We are bound by the sacraments, but *God* is not bound. Jesus does not sit on his hands refusing to work in our lives till we ask him to be our personal Savior any more than he is helpless to act unless we are baptized. Our very ability to seek him is already fruit of his grace. God works through sacraments, most assuredly. But sacraments are given as sure encounters with grace, not as reducing valves designed to make sure the unbaptized are excluded from God.

Christ also comes to us through innumerable creatures, since all creation is sacramental. One of the sacramentals bringing us Christ is our neighbor—especially the least of our neighbors. For the stunning truth is that Christ is present in all those you meet. How you treat them is how you treat him. And how you treat them is not merely "spiritual" (that is, with attention to their souls but none to their stomachs, wardrobe, or housing situation). A plumber who fixes a single mom's sink at no charge does as much a work of Christ (and for Christ) as the priest who hears her confession or gives her the Eucharist. If you cooperate with grace, you are Christ's hands and heart in the world and a gift of grace to your neighbor. Likewise, your neighbor—especially your poor neighbor—is God's gift to you, a sacramental through whom Christ works in your soul.

That's why the parable of the sheep and the goats does not remotely contradict the Catholic sacramental vision. Saying that God comes to us in the person of a beggar is not saying God does *not* come to us in the Sacrament of the Altar.

It is, however, an emphatic denial that God saves by faith alone. Archbishop Charles Chaput of Philadelphia summed up the Church's attitude toward this notion quite bluntly when he stated, "If we ignore the poor, we will go to hell."[4] Faith alone won't cut it if you send a starving waif back out in the snow saying, "Go in peace, be warmed and filled" (James 2:16).

That's breathtaking—like a punch in the gut. But that's what the parable of the sheep and the goats means. The shocked sheep, like the shocked goats, may or may not have had all sorts of theological theories about salvation by faith alone or "once saved, always saved" or the efficacy of the sacraments. What they found, however, was that the king said, "Truly, I say to you, as you did it to one of the least of these my brethren, you did it to me" (Matthew 25:40).

That is a tonic reminder of the Church's ancient tradition of the corporal and spiritual works of mercy. It is also a vital lesson for those who hold false OSAS theories. The corporal works of mercy pertain to the deeds mentioned in the parable of the sheep and the goats as well as to a couple of other precepts of Jewish and Christian civility and goodness done in the love of God. They are:

Feed the hungry
Give drink to the thirsty
Clothe the naked
Harbor the harborless
Visit the sick
Ransom the captive
Bury the dead

The spiritual works of mercy, while not mentioned in the parable, nonetheless reflect biblical teaching about the love of God for our wretched race. They are the mother of all the hospitals, schools, and other acts of sheer kindness the Church has birthed over the centuries. They are:

Instruct the ignorant
Counsel the doubtful
Admonish sinners
Bear wrongs patiently
Forgive offenses willingly

Comfort the afflicted

Pray for the living and the dead

The spiritual works of mercy are ordered toward the fact that merely relieving physical need, while itself a very good thing, is not enough, because we are human beings. One of the basic mistakes of communism (and capitalism in our increasingly de-Christianized culture) is to regard people as creatures motivated solely by the same instincts that motivate an animal. The idea is that both cows and people need to eat, breathe, work, excrete, and have sex, so a civilization that makes these activities the highest goals is a civilization that has all the bases covered. It is a huge mistake remedied by a simple observation: namely, that animals, in the absence of biological opportunity, go to sleep, whereas humans get bored and restless. Why? Because our spirits cry out for more than eating, breathing, working, excreting, and having sex. We are not mere beasts. We are rational creatures in the image of God who long for union with him. The spiritual works of mercy are founded on the knowledge that man does not live "by bread alone, but by every word that proceeds from the mouth of God" (Matthew 4:4).

In this book we will therefore take a look at the corporal and spiritual works of mercy in order to see how to incarnate our faith in works of love for God and neighbor, so that we may, as 2 Peter 1:10 says, make our calling and election sure and, in union with our Lord Jesus, help renew the face of the earth.

CHAPTER 1

Feed the Hungry

*N*ORMAN BORLAUG IS NOT THE sort of name you think of when it comes to world-historical heroism. A Norwegian Lutheran son of Iowa, he grew up on the prairie, went to college during the Depression, studied the thoroughly unglamorous subject of agriculture, enjoyed wrestling, met his wife while waiting tables at a university Dinkytown coffee shop where they both worked, and had three kids. He never starred in a movie, never ran for office, never led men into battle, and would not have been noticeable to you if you saw him in the street.

Oh yeah, and he saved the lives of a billion people.

Norman Borlaug was the father of the Green Revolution, an awesome scientific undertaking of twentieth-century American agricultural science that resulted in the breeding of fantastically fruitful strains of food plants that kept the burgeoning population of the world (especially the Third World) from starving to death. Almost nobody has heard of him owing to the characteristic modesty of his generation and cultural background, but without him we could well be living in a postapocalyptic nightmare.

That nightmare was sketched for us in 1968 by a self-anointed prophet named Paul Ehrlich, who knew everything except what he was talking about. In his book *The Population Bomb*, Ehrlich set the pace still followed by our culture of death when he embraced the Malthusian approach to the problem of feeding humanity by curling up in a ball, proclaiming defeat, and saying with Scrooge, "If the poor be like to die, they had better do it and help decrease the surplus population." As Ehrlich put it, "The battle to feed all of humanity is over.... In the 1970s and 1980s hundreds of millions of people will starve to death in spite of any crash programs embarked upon now." He added, "I have yet to meet anyone familiar with the situation who thinks India will be self-sufficient in food by 1971," and "India couldn't possibly feed two hundred million more people by 1980."[1]

The prophet of doom didn't reckon on Norman Borlaug, whose new strains of plants produced enormous yields that doubled India's food production, made Mexico a grain exporter, and saved the lives of a billion people throughout the world.

When Ehrlich dies, I sincerely hope that this apostle of defeat and contraception will not hear the words spoken to the servant who hid his one talent in the ground (see Matthew 25:14–30). But I am confident that if anybody stands a good chance of hearing from Jesus, "I was hungry and you gave me food," it will be Norman Borlaug, who goes down in history, without any possible comparison, as the guy who gave more food to the "least of these" than anybody who ever lived. We can certainly pray with hope that when he died on September 9, 2009, he heard (perhaps with the same surprise as the sheep in the parable), "Come, O blessed of my Father, inherit the kingdom prepared for you from the foundation of the world" (Matthew 25:34).

Borlaug symbolizes one pole of a dynamic tension that always exists in the Catholic tradition: the tension between practical results and good intentions. The woman at the temple treasury who put in two small copper coins is at the other pole (see Luke 21:1–3). In terms of "results," they couldn't be further apart. The woman could barely feed herself, much less the world. Nonetheless, the two have something in common: They did the most they could with what they had. Borlaug used his gifts and exploited his opportunities in order to feed a billion people. The woman at the treasury put in "all the living that she had"—and it counted more in God's sight than all the gifts that the rich gave from their excess.

Most of us live somewhere between these two great heroes, but all of us are called to do the best we can with what we have. For us average Catholics, this usually means we schlep along, supporting charities, making sure that company is fed when they visit, perhaps working in our parish soup kitchen—trying to give a little bit extra. That's not a thing to be sneezed at. Not all have the gift and calling to found some gigantic ministry that feeds the poor. But lots of us can (and do) give our tithe and then some to those who do have such a calling. Mercy Corps, Food for the Poor, Feed the Children, and a boatload of other organizations wouldn't exist if *everybody* was a visionary inspired to create some multinational organization to help the starving masses. Such organizations require masses of ordinary folk like you and me to pour in our little copper coins faithfully according to our means so they can do their great work.

Result: American charitable giving in 2009 was $303.75 billion. That's the third year in a row that charitable giving had exceeded 300 billion dollars—during the worst economic downturn since the Depression. This clearly shows how the ordinary, commonplace ethic of Christian charity is one of the most vital lubricants to the smooth running of our civilization. Getting rid of the faith while expecting its fruits to continue is but one of the many lunatic ideas the New Atheists advocate as they look forward to a culture running on reason alone. But anybody can see that charity is not according to reason. It is according to love, which is a higher thing than mere reason and addresses human beings as higher things than mere animals or ingredients in an economic formula. Lord alone knows how many social upheavals have been prevented because ordinary people took it upon themselves to buy a down-and-out guy a cup of coffee or help a young mother move into her apartment or just spend an hour on a park bench listening to a lonely bore. It is impossible to calculate the good that has been done by the works of charity the Christian tradition encourages. And in a certain sense, all of them could be seen as "feeding the hungry."

For of course, "feeding the hungry" means more than feeding the belly. Man does not live by bread alone but by every word that proceeds from the mouth of God. At this very hour, billions are starving for meaning as much as, indeed more than, they starve for bread. Whole societies and civilizations that have the bottom of Maslow's pyramid[2] covered are empty to the core because, as the sacred writer says, "Where there is no vision, the people perish" (Proverbs 29:18, *KJV*). Our McDonaldized culture has the problem of hunger largely licked (with a few exceptions). Indeed, the poor in our culture have much more to fear from obesity and diabetes than from dying in the snows like Hans Christian Andersen's Little Match Girl.

We will talk of that more, particularly when we discuss the spiritual works of mercy. But before we rush off to spiritualize things safely into the realm of the noneconomic, let's stick, for the time being, to the subject of feeding the hungry with real, physical food. While the poor here in America may be struggling with obesity, abroad it is another story, as millions are still in literal danger of starving to death. Is this because (as Euro-American population planners continually tell us) we have just enough of us white people but way too many brown ones? No, it's because the starving people live under evil, man-made socioeconomic and political systems that prevent food, of which there is more than enough in the world, from reaching their hungry bellies. Instead it gets bottled up somewhere or turned to an unjust profit for some despot who loves gold and grinds the face of the poor.

The solution is not to tell the poor person to kill his child so that we rich Westerners can have carbon credits. It is to demand that the rich Westerner, Third World tyrant, or exploitative corporate system give the poor man what is rightly his: enough food to eat. This is not Marxism. Indeed, it is not even a "work of mercy." This is Church teaching on mere justice:

> St. John Chrysostom vigorously recalls this: "Not to enable the poor to share in our goods is to steal from them and deprive them of life. The goods we possess are not ours, but theirs." "The demands of justice must be satisfied first of all;

that which is already due in justice is not to be offered as a gift of charity":

> When we attend to the needs of those in want, we give them what is theirs, not ours. More than performing works of mercy, we are paying a debt of justice.[3]

Perhaps a better way to phrase that is "Less than performing works of mercy, we are paying a debt of justice." For of course, mere acts of justice are not superabundant works of mercy; they are the bare minimum expected of us as functional moral beings. Obeying the Ten Commandments is not heroism; it's the very least we can expect. The Ten Commandments essentially say, "If you can't love your neighbor, at least don't beat him to death with a baseball bat, steal his stuff, or run off with his wife." Similarly, Jesus tells us:

> If you love those who love you, what reward have you? Do not even the tax collectors do the same? And if you salute only your brethren, what more are you doing than others? Do not even the Gentiles do the same? (Matthew 5:46–47).

Merely doing the just thing, then, is not really the goal. Merely not robbing the poor of what is rightfully theirs is not heroic sanctity. What is called for is not mere fairness but love that goes above and beyond.

I don't like hearing that any more than you do. I feel the economic pinch too. I fret, as do you, about how much I can afford to go the extra mile and give generously. And truth be told, I sometimes cut corners.

But for all my faults and hypocrisy, the simple fact is, I'm not making this stuff up. I didn't invent the tradition. I merely report it. And the tradition has always been emphatic: Feed the hungry to the best of your ability.

Don't make much? Feed the hungry anyway, even if it's just a bit.

Do you, like me, battle the temptation to eat like a pig and often find yourself losing ground? Feed the hungry and kick yourself for your failures afterward.

Resentful of the shiftless poor? Jesus didn't say, "Feed the deserving." He just said, "Feed the hungry."

Peter, do you love me? Then feed the hungry! If your name is not Peter, do it anyway.

We are to feed the hungry for two basic reasons that I can detect in the Catholic tradition. First, because the hungry are hungry, and second, because the hungry are Jesus. Medieval thinkers understood the idea that we know lesser truths more surely and greater truths less surely, just as we can see a candle clearly but not the sun. Similarly, the way we know we have fed the hungry is when they burp and pat their tummies. The way we know we have fed Jesus is purely because he tells us it is so. It is a classic example of the way God supernaturally reveals things we could not possibly know on our own. The presence of Jesus Christ in the poor is no more evident to the senses than is the presence of Jesus Christ in the Holy Eucharist. It is purely a matter of faith in his word.

And indeed, one of the ironies of our present culture of New Atheist hostility to the Faith is that those who routinely sneer at the Real Presence in the Eucharist imagine that once faith is gone, we will see the dignity of the poor more clearly. This delusion will, in fact, vanish should the faith really be excised as people like Richard Dawkins, Sam Harris, and Christopher Hitchens wish. Without the dignity Jesus gives the poor, the first response of an icy rationalist will be to judge the poor on the empirical evidence alone: the smell of alcohol, pot, urine, and vomit; the schizophrenic rambling; the addictions; the violence; the ignorance; the ratty clothes, toothlessness, and appalling hygiene; the child abuse—all clusters of social, economic, and psychological pathologies that swarm around the poor like maggots. These will be the only "facts" about them. Their dignity will be dismissed as mere sentimental projection, a holdover from the bad old days when people believed all that superstitious Jesus junk. And the quick, easy, and rational response of a society that has been carefully instructed to dismiss the presence of Christ from its mind will be not charity but the same solution that cold clinicians always propose—namely, to cull the herd of the unfit and eliminate contagion from the breed. Should Christianity ever successfully be extirpated from the public square, expect the extermination of the poor, not their exaltation.

Against this, the faith has always proposed the wildly impractical fact that Jesus really is present in the poor as (in a different mode) he is present in the Eucharist. Therefore we must feed the hungry or face the doom: "Depart from me, you cursed, into the eternal fire prepared for the devil and his angels; for I was hungry and you gave me no food" (Matthew 25:41–42).

The demand of Jesus to feed the hungry is challengingly open-ended. In a world of starving people, our tradition says to live within our means, take care of our families—and be as generous as God. A terrifying prospect. "Love your *enemies*.... Be *perfect as your heavenly Father is perfect*" (Matthew 5:44, 48, emphasis mine). In a word, do not act from Minimum Daily Adult Requirement stinginess, which asks, "What's the least generosity I can get away with and still make the cut?" Instead, like Christ, ask, "How can I give my life away in love for God?"

I have no clear program for that any more than most people do, so I toss in my little copper coins as I can. I have my charities I support, as do you.[4] I pray that when I share my worldly goods, it will be enough to help and that Jesus will receive it. I ask for light, and when our Lord sees fit, he gives it.

I'm also aware that there is no resting on laurels when it comes to works of mercy. God's project of salvation is so crazy and huge that only he could attempt it. We puny mortals chip in our two bits and help a family here and there with a gift. Now and then some bright meteor like Norman Borlaug pitches in and dramatically rescues a billion souls. Meanwhile, we live in hope that our faith will be honored where our ability to save a billion lives is lacking. After all, Jesus was able to do a lot with five loaves and two fishes.

CHAPTER | 2

Give Drink to the Thirsty

A RELIGION THAT PRACTICES BAPTISM is a religion that doesn't have very rigorous membership requirements. No Herculean feats necessary to prove your mettle. No ritual bath in bull's blood. No gashing yourself with knives or holding your hand over an open flame to attest to your commitment. No proof is necessary beyond your word that you mean to try to be a good Christian. Just a splash of water three times, a few ritual words, and you are good to go!

You don't even need to possess the faculty of consciousness if you happen to be born into a Catholic family: Mom and Dad do that bit for you till you are ready to claim the faith for your own when you reach the age of reason. The baptismal water runs off your velvety newborn head, and the gift of eternal life is granted by our profligate God. It's as though Catholics really believe all that stuff about salvation by grace and not by hard work on our part!

In light of this, water is once again seen as a fitting symbol of the grace of God. Three-quarters of the earth's surface is covered by the stuff that first mediates the sacramental grace of God to us. Most of the human body is made of it. It's Adam's ale, the most common thing in the world—like grace.

Some folks react to that last sentence as though it were a slam on the grace of God. How dare I call it "common"? But that's only because some folks think that calling something common is the same as calling it "cheap" or "boring" or "unimportant."

Not so. The most important things in the world are common. Breathing, for instance. You don't think about it while you exercise the privilege, but let somebody interrupt it for just a few seconds and your appreciation for it shows a marked uptick.

Love is common. People are constantly falling in love. And it is exquisite every time, a little gleam of heaven.

Birth is common. And every birth is a miracle.

Death is common. And every death is a tiny Golgotha in which another human being is joined to the sufferings of the Son of God and his Blessed Mother.

The commonness of water is like those common—and precious—things. Consider: The sheep in the parable are marked by the fact that they gave Jesus something to drink. That doesn't *seem* very reward-worthy. It's not exactly up there with slaying the Hydra or battling an army grown from dragon's teeth or cleaning the Augean stables. When we go to a restaurant and a waiter gives us our customary glass of ice water, we do not break forth in alleluias. When a man mows the grass and his wife gives him a glass of water, we do not customarily rejoice that salvation has visited that house. Yet Jesus chooses *this* image as a sign of our worthiness for heaven. What gives?

At this point it is often customary for the imagination to wander to scenes we are sure we recall from the Bible somewhere, like that time Jesus gave a drink of water to the desperately parched Charlton Heston in 1 Wyler 10:42.[1] But it turns out that scene is from *Ben Hur*, not Scripture. In scenes like *that*, we can certainly see how giving somebody a cup of cold water might be commendable as an act of mercy.

But how often do we have occasion to meet desperately thirsty chain gangs full of innocents, much less have an artesian well nearby when we do? Indeed, if it comes to that, how often, even in Jesus' day, was the average person confronted with forced marches of parched criminals to whom he could dramatically give drink? Perhaps such things happened with a little more frequency under the Roman boot than in suburban America. But as a rule, it was not common. So this leaves us somewhat at a loss as to how to *implement* this teaching in our life, as well as with a puzzle about how such a saying would have been understood by Jesus' disciples. Desperate thirst, while it certainly could occur in a world without indoor plumbing and at the mercy of drought, was not all *that* normal an occurrence.

This is not, by the way, to say that there's no problem with the water supply in human habitats the world over, either then or today. As charities such as Global Water attest, there is much to be done to assure that people in the Third World have a source of clean, safe water to drink. Likewise, as initiatives like the Nestlé boycott attest, the parable of Lazarus and the rich man is still being played out today, only the rich man is now busy profiteering off the thirst of Lazarus by telling his mother, "Don't feed your boy with that low-tech breast milk! Instead, line *our* pockets by using this snazzy new formula that you mix with contaminated water! Sure, your kid will be between six and twenty-five times more likely to die of diarrhea and four times more likely to die of pneumonia than a breast-fed child, but that's a small price to pay for making me richer!"

That said, it's still worth asking how the command to give drink to the thirsty might have been understood by Jesus' hearers. Charities such as Global Water and corporations such as Nestlé did not exist when Jesus spoke. Those who heard him were not thinking about the problem of dysentery in Sudanese water supplies a thousand miles from their village in Galilee. So while we do well to consider such matters and do our part to help ensure that an African mother is not bamboozled into killing her child by corporate hucksters eager to make a buck, we also need to consider what this passage may have meant to those who first read it.

It is worth noting that when the early Christians thought about thirst—and especially the thirst of "the least of these my brethren" —there was one thing they could readily connect these sayings to:

> After this Jesus, knowing that all was now finished, said (to fulfil the Scripture), "I thirst." A bowl full of vinegar stood there; so they put a sponge full of the vinegar on hyssop and held it to his mouth. (John 19:28–29)

Jesus had thirsted. He had thirsted physically on the cross—an intense burning thirst brought on by massive loss of body fluids following his scourging. When he begged for drink, our wretched race gave him vinegar. And his followers got much the same treatment:

crucified, stoned, cut to ribbons, roasted alive on spits. The torments we devised for the least of his brethren just goes on and on.

In this light, the cup of cold water comes back into focus as a humble and sharp rebuke to human cruelty and selfishness. So small an act as this is impossible for the fallen human creature in the grip of Christ hatred. Indeed, it can, under the right conditions of mob mood, even mark you as "the wrong sort": a sympathizer and fellow traveler who deserves the same fate as did Jesus. Just as Peter could imagine the hot breath of condemnation on his neck for the crime of having an accent similar to his (see Mark 14:70), so even the smallest act of perceived connection to Jesus can cost you your neck when the world is in the mood to persecute.

However, such is the divine generosity that even so small an act of charity to his saints can be what carries us into God's light when the final reckoning comes. That is, I suspect, the meaning of this passage:

> He who receives you receives me, and he who receives me receives him who sent me. He who receives a prophet because he is a prophet shall receive a prophet's reward, and he who receives a righteous man because he is a righteous man shall receive a righteous man's reward. And whoever gives to one of these little ones even a cup of cold water because he is a disciple, truly, I say to you, he shall not lose his reward. (Matthew 10:40–42)

To give drink to the thirsty in this context is to give drink to Christ himself, panting in desperation in the person of some helpless soul chased by a mob or harried into hiding by a pogrom. To be kind to a disciple fleeing persecution or to take in an apostle as a guest was, indeed, to give food and drink to Christ, as the Philippian jailer discovered when he welcomed Paul and Silas (see Acts 16:16–40).

But above all, to give drink to the thirsty would, in the mind of the early Church, most certainly have been connected with the gift of living water. Preaching the gospel in Rome or most of the urbanized areas subject to Caesar, in the shadow of the aqueducts, one would have been hard pressed to find bodies dying of thirst. But one could find a plentiful supply of souls hungering and thirsting after righteousness. To them the parable of the sheep and the goats would have been inevitably joined to the story of the Samaritan woman:

> There came a woman of Samaria to draw water. Jesus said to her, "Give me a drink." For his disciples had gone away into the city to buy food. The Samaritan woman said to him, "How is it that you, a Jew, ask a drink of me, a woman of Samaria?" For Jews have no dealings with Samaritans. Jesus answered her, "If you knew the gift of God, and who it is that is saying to you, 'Give me a drink,' / you would have asked him, and he would have given you living water." / The woman said to him, "Sir, you have nothing to draw with, and the well is deep; where do you get that living water? Are you greater than our father Jacob, who gave us the well, and drank from it himself, and his sons, and his cattle?" Jesus said to her, "Every one who drinks of this water will thirst again, but whoever drinks of the water that I shall give him will never thirst; the water that I shall give him will become in

him a spring of water welling up to eternal life." (John
4:7–14)

To give drink to the thirsty is now, as it was then, a supreme work of
mercy in that it involves giving the living water of the Spirit to those
who cry out for him. To be sure, the bodily needs of the thirsty must
be met. But because human beings are not brute beasts, they need
more than this. They suffer from a thirst that no earthly water can
satisfy. Indeed, as many an addict will tell you, it is a thirst that men
have destroyed their lives seeking to quench with mortal elixirs
promising life and delivering death. That is why the water at Jacob's
well—and indeed all the water in the world—could not slake the
Samaritan woman's thirst. Only Jesus can give us that water. And in
the end it is only by this common yet miraculous drink that we can
fully and truly give drink to the thirsty.

CHAPTER | 3

Clothe the Naked

*N*AKE IS AN EXTINCT ENGLISH verb meaning "to strip clothes off." To be "naked" is therefore to be in a state of having had your clothes stripped off.

Why does this bit of pedantry matter? Because it speaks volumes about what our ancestors regarded as the natural state of man. While a couple of loopy groups attempted it in warmer Mediterranean climates in early Christendom, it is not until after the Reformation, the rise of the Enlightenment, and especially the rise of technologies that allow northern Europeans to maintain a bit of comfiness in chill weather that we started to see the rise of so-called Adamite movements (later frankly renamed "nudist"), which propose that our natural state is to walk around buck naked. The theory that clothes are an unnatural encumbrance on our glorious childlike freedom is an illusion that only technology and warm weather permit us to entertain.

For our ancestors of not many generations back, such a proposal was not just silly in a practical sense; it was also about 180 degrees from normality. Fallen man was, so to speak, born clothed. Something unnatural had to be done—he had to undergo some process of *naking*—for him to end up naked. It was seen not as a return to simplicity and beauty but as a shameful state. Pity—or scorn, never breezy flower-child approval—was heaped on those found naked.

The vast majority of sensible people have not been sophisticated out of this basic insight. It's why there are separate men's and women's restrooms, and even in those we have separate stalls so we do not have to expose ourselves to strangers. It's why people revolt against TSA scanners stripping travelers naked electronically. It's why comic sketches, movies, and bawdy stories often feature a man caught in public without his pants or a woman similarly caught without her clothes. It's why the Nazis, in addition to murdering their victims, savored the extra cruelty of first forcing them to strip naked. It's why the Son of God was stripped naked by the agents of Satan as he hung on the cross. To *nake* someone, to strip him or her publicly, is universally understood as taking away that person's human dignity. Clothes, in some mystical sense, quite literally make the man.

Of course, culturally relative issues crowd in on this insight. Martha Washington and, say, the San people of the Kalahari have altogether different ideas of what "being dressed" means. Moses' notions of what constituted shameful dress differ markedly from those of my twenty-first-century wife padding around the garden in her jeans. (Deuteronomy 22:5—"A woman shall not wear anything that pertains to a man, nor shall a man put on a woman's garment; for whoever does these things is an abomination to the LORD your God.")

Libertines and puritans have great fun with these cultural differences, jockeying either to eradicate the virtue of modesty or to raise fashion sense to the granite standards of Sinai, in any case oversimplifying the complex interplay of aesthetics, common sense, and morality. Puritans are dead certain they can define good and evil clothing and which movements of a button or hemline mark the flight from righteousness to sin. Libertines are quite certain that any thought concerning the symbolic function of clothing is puritanical. This is all of a piece with the sort of easy libertine relativism that attempts to say, "People dispute whether you can have one wife or several, so why bother with marriage?" or "People quibble about what constitutes just war, so do whatever it takes to win."

In fact, however, the first thing to note about the diversity of views on clothing is that, while many argue about what clothes are proper, *everybody normally wears some kind of clothes.* That's why nudists are in colonies and not in your street. It may be only a loincloth or a string of beads, but the thing that marks *Homo sapiens* off from the rest of the animal kingdom is that people wear clothes, even when there is no need for warmth or protection.

This gives the lie to the notion that Genesis 1–3 is somehow the cause of a religion of shame about the body. In reality, Genesis accounts for a phenomenon as old as humanity and as common among Hottentots, ancient Druids, and Japanese as it is among Jews and Christians: the fact that humans feel the deep psychological need to be clothed and avoid public naking, except in very specifically prescribed cultural and social ritual situations. A Roman might be at ease in the public baths without a stitch on. But it doesn't follow that he strolled home that way. Archimedes may have leapt from the tub and run screaming "Eureka!" through the streets buck naked, but the reason we know the story today is because this was just as unconventional to Greeks and Romans as streakers at a ball game are to us today.

Because clothes have so very much to do with our human dignity, Jesus urges us to clothe the naked. But this confronts us with a problem. As with every counsel of Jesus, the command to clothe the naked has both a practical and a spiritual dimension, because grace builds on nature. Here's the rub: My encounters with the naked beggar are fairly rare, as are yours. The people I meet in the soup-kitchen line at Blessed Sacrament parish in Seattle are not naked. Nor are the homeless folk you meet in your town. Once again, we live in a society where the bottom of Maslow's pyramid is pretty well covered. In the First World the purely animal need for insulating cloth in which to enwrap the human organism is pretty well covered. Clothing banks swell to bursting with free clothing of every size. Rare indeed is the opportunity for us in the First World to live out Jesus' command, "If any one would sue you and take your coat, let him have your cloak as well" (Matthew 5:40).

However, if we cast our view further abroad, we discover that this is not the case universally. At this hour, many millions of Lazaruses around the world sit naked or nearly naked because they cannot afford clothes. The ragged clothes they have—infested with maggots and insects and covered with their own blood, pus, and vomit—are their only shield against the elements and shame. Each one of these is Jesus Christ. Clothe him and you have clothed the Son of the living God, who will not forget it on that Day.

Other considerations enter in too. On the one hand, clothes symbolize our external lives—the junk that doesn't matter in the end. So Jesus tells us that the body is more than clothes (see Luke 12:23). But on the other hand, clothes also express the heart of the wearer. In the parable of the wedding banquet, the sinner was thrown out because he neglected to wear the wedding garment (Matthew 22:1–14). In Scripture you should not show up for a feast in rags, but neither would you wear rich apparel instead of sackcloth and ashes when you fast.

In short, clothes are never *merely* clothes. They *mean.* They express. Clothes are also extensions of ourselves, and they can even be sacramental. In the Old Testament there is, for instance, enormous attention paid to the clothing of the high priest—because clothing *speaks.* For similar reasons Paul tells us:

> Let us then cast off the works of darkness and put on the armor of light; let us conduct ourselves becomingly as in the day, not in reveling and drunkenness, not in debauchery and licentiousness, not in quarreling and jealousy. But put on the Lord Jesus Christ, and make no provision for the flesh, to gratify its desires. (Romans 13:12–14)

And so the Church tells the newly baptized, "You have become a new creation, and have clothed yourself in Christ. See in this white garment the outward sign of your Christian dignity."[1]

This is easy to misapply, as European missionaries did in reasoning, "We are from Christian Europe, while these Africans are savages." This thinking resulted in some of the silliest acts of colonialism:

Africans forced to abandon their own customary clothing and wear nineteenth-century frock coats and top hats in equatorial Africa. Much can be made of such folly, and the enemies of the Church's missionary enterprise have not hesitated to do so. But these same enemies of evangelization think nothing of imposing on the entire Third World one particular piece of clothing called the condom.

Indeed, the First World labors with might and main to fill the Third World with Madonna T-shirts, Nike shoes, and the rest of the output of a post-Christian consumer culture in a manner every bit as colonial as that of Victorian England. It's just that the colonizers are now corporations instead of nation-states. The tendency of Euro-American culture to impose itself on the world is as vibrant now as a century ago, but what that culture now regards as the highest good is no longer God and country but consumerist, hedonist, democratic capitalism.

What is more, the First World has largely succeeded in these efforts. For all the maundering heard in politically correct circles about the horrors of the Church allegedly eradicating native cultures, one seldom sees Chinese diplomats speaking before the UN in seventeenth-century Chinese garb, untouched by Western fashion trends. Visit New Zealand and the Maori will be cheerfully dressed in jeans and T-shirts; they're not pining for precolonial Maori fashion. You don't bump into Chinese women with bound feet (thank God), and the guys who run the gigantic, gaudy casino on the Indian reservation a few miles north of me have sartorial tastes that run more toward Gucci and less toward Chief Sealth. In a global economy, it turns out that people prefer what's cheap, comfortable, and trendy over the solemn preservation of their own indigenous culture. It may be a loss, but it's a loss as old as Joseph's willingness to abandon his Semitic fashion choices for the clothes, perfumes, and makeup of the Egyptian elite (see Genesis 37–47).

All this is to say that, while we are commanded to clothe the naked, the Church largely leaves it up to us and our very loosey-goosey sense of what is appropriate when it comes to how we are to do that. The Church seeks "enculturation": affirming what is good and natural in local customs of dress but calling us away from immodesty and depravity in that matter as in others. Missionaries in the Church's history (like Matteo Ricci) adopted the approach of wearing whatever the locals were wearing. Others have thought it necessary to define *naked* not as "lacking clothes" but as "lacking *modest* clothes." In our sexually deranged post-Christian culture, it is easy to dismiss such people as cultural imperialists while forgetting that some of this thinking is directed not at "savages" but, quite justifiably, at our own culture.

One can, for instance, question the wisdom of clothing seven-year-olds as slatterns and sending them out in public to perform "Single Ladies."[2] Technically, the children who performed that dance were "clothed." Indeed, they had more clothes on than a San tribesman on the Kalahari. But in the grammar of fashion as it is spoken in the West, the message was "Show me a culture that despises virginity, and I'll show you a culture that despises childhood innocence." Such a display aims not to clothe the naked but to come as close as possible to naking the clothed for the delectation of perverts. We needn't be shocked that such a culture produces vast quantities of child porn.

Clothing, like all things human, is not something you can reduce to mere materialism, any more than the words on this page can be adequately understood only as black marks on white paper. Clothes have a language and grammar that speak in highly particular cultural contexts. We must understand that language and grammar as we clothe the naked, just as we must understand the language and grammar of food as we feed the hungry. Nobody wears mere clothes, just as nobody eats mere food. Offering bacon to a starving Jew in Auschwitz is not a work of charity but adds insult to injury. Giving a saltine cracker to a birthday child instead of a cake does not say, "I love you."

As a general rule, the command to clothe the naked is concerned primarily not with the need for human warmth but with the need for human dignity. Our task as Catholics is to clothe the naked in accord with the prevailing cultural "grammar" of virtue and to acknowledge human dignity thereby. It is to remember that clothes were made for man, not man for clothes—and that, above all, we are to

> put off the old man with his practices and ... put on the new man, who is being renewed in knowledge after the image of his creator. Here there cannot be Greek and Jew, circumcised and uncircumcised, barbarian, Scythian, slave, free man, but Christ is all, and in all.
>
> Put on then, as God's chosen ones, holy and beloved, compassion, kindness, lowliness, meekness, and patience, forbearing one another and, if one has a complaint against another, forgiving each other; as the Lord has forgiven you, so you also must forgive. And over all these put on love, which binds everything together in perfect harmony. (Colossians 3:9–14)

CHAPTER | 4

Harbor the Harborless

ONE OF THE MOST EXASPERATING bits of exegetical trendiness to afflict First World Catholics for the past thirty years or so has been the endless recirculation, like that of a bad penny, of the "True Meaning of the Miracle of the Loaves and Fishes" homily. It goes like this:

Jesus found himself in the wilderness with a crowd of five thousand people who were two millennia stupider than we smart suburban Americans. When people started getting hungry, Jesus took five loaves and two fishes and gave them to a couple of people around him. Suddenly, inspired by a wave of warm fuzziness emanating from this gesture, everybody remembered the picnic baskets they had tucked away in the folds of their robes and started sharing their lunches. People were so moved by this utterly unprecedented outburst of mutual generosity that they called it the "miracle" of the loaves and fishes. So we should also likewise share our lunches. The End.

It's a story that only suburban Americans could possibly believe. As a Palestinian friend of mine once said, "My father would sooner see our family starve to *death* than that a guest should go without food." That's a sentiment found almost universally in the hospitality of the Near East, and it has roots that go back to remotest antiquity. The notion that Jesus "inspired" ancient Semites to share their food in the miracle of the loaves and fishes is as preposterous as the notion that he "inspired" them to walk on two legs or breathe air for the first time in their history. It's balderdash. Hospitality was one of the sacred duties universally recognized by everybody in the crowd that day.

Indeed, the Old Testament is full of testimony to the ancient Jewish conviction that care for guests was crucial. Abraham, for instance, is marked by his sense of hospitality, most notably when the three visitors arrive to promise the birth of Isaac and to warn of the destruction of Sodom (see Genesis 18). Scripture constantly emphasizes Israel's duty of hospitality to the alien, the orphan, and the widow (see, for example, Deuteronomy 10:18 and Leviticus 19:34). The book of Ruth centers on the duty to take in strangers—and it becomes a book of the Bible because out of this drama issues Israel's greatest king, David, a descendent of Ruth.

David's story, of course, ultimately issues in the birth of the Son of David, Jesus. Yet the paradox of Jesus' birth is that "his own received him not" (John 1:11, *KJV*). He was shunted off to a stable to be born. He lived the life of an itinerant preacher with nowhere to lay his head. His few moments with a roof over his head were unusual, and those who (such as Mary of Bethany) provided him with hospitality are remembered for it. He died despised and rejected of men, and even his burial place had to be borrowed since he had none of his own.

This is the backdrop for the Christian understanding of the tradition of hospitality—a tradition that both ennobles and bedevils us. It's the source of that great Christian invention, the "hospital" (note the etymology of the word) and of the current chaos in our country concerning illegal immigration. It's why we give to homeless shelters and why we feel so baffled and conflicted by the homeless when we meet them. Do we tell them, "If any one will not work, let him not eat," as did St. Paul (2 Thessalonians 3:10), or take them in, as Mother Teresa would do?

The Church, as is her custom, does not offer us a program for harboring the harborless any more than she writes us a recipe book to buttress her command to feed the hungry. It's pretty much up to us how we are to live out the ideal. So, for instance, some people start—and many people support—homeless shelters, shelters for runaways, shelters for battered women and drug addicts, and so forth. Others (with more courage than most of us, including me) take homeless people into their homes. This is radical charity. It is also quite dangerous, as a woman I know discovered when her grateful guests fled the premises with her wallet and embarked on a campaign of identity theft that has yet to reach its end.

This brings us to a point many well-meaning people discover in painful ways: Just because somebody is a victim doesn't mean they can't be bad too. Hitler, after all, was homeless once. It's easy, in the flush of excitement over conversion, to leap into a Franciscan zeal for the homeless, only to discover that the homeless guy you want to help is homeless not because he's one of the wretched of the earth to whom fate dealt a bad hand but because he's a violent, unstable parasite who bites the hand that feeds him. Sometimes the bum suffers not from bum luck but from sitting on his sinful bum. Sometimes it really is better to let professionals handle things than to assume that your sanctity will melt the heart of the guy who, unbeknownst to you, is wanted for rape in three states.

Yet we are commanded to harbor the harborless. We can become personally involved, and we can supply financial support. For instance, a small nondenominational church in Seattle started sponsoring refugees in the 1980s. I remember it well because it was my church. Our pastor arranged with a relief agency to help a Vietnamese family who had survived Pol Pot's Killing Fields. We also sponsored families from communist Romania and communist Poland.

That's not just an Evangelical thing. Catholics can do it too, especially Catholic parishes that pool their considerable resources.

Of course, in keeping with Chesterton's famous remark that Catholics agree about everything and only disagree about everything else, it's worth noting that the question of just how to harbor the harborless has no one-size-fits-all approach. The American episcopacy (and many priests and lay Catholics) are all over the map concerning how the Church should respond to illegal immigrants. Some of the confusion is due to the fact that the question of how the Church should respond is not the same as the question of how Caesar should respond. A priest in Los Angeles is not bound by the question of whether the human being at his door is legal. He is bound by the fact that the human being at his door is Jesus Christ.

At the same time, foolish things have been said to the effect that

America is like Nazi Germany for so much as having an immigration policy. This is silly. Every state needs a way of screening out dangers to the common good. So trying to create a workable system of legal immigration is just common sense. No nation on earth has been as welcoming of the stranger as the United States has—a testimony to the penetration of this particular corporal work of mercy into the American psyche. How the struggle over immigration policy will play out, I do not know. But if we follow our historical pattern, we can hope that the stranger from the south will find a welcome as did the stranger from Ireland, southern Europe, and Asia.

Meanwhile, it is not the task of most of us to deal with twelve million illegal aliens. Instead, we can start in much simpler ways by welcoming strangers, whether the literally homeless or the spiritually lonely ones within our own parishes. In my experience, that's where we lay Catholics can be of huge assistance to the body of Christ.

Spiritual homelessness in one's own parish is endemic in Catholic America. All over the United States, average Catholics sit as strangers in the pews. "Nobody knows my name. We have no friends here. I come to get my sacrament card punched each Sunday, but I have no living connection to this parish." Such stories of aching loneliness are heard again and again in parishes around the country. It's the number-one reason ex-Catholics are ex-Catholics. It's not because of a theological excuse that gets layered on later, such as having read the words "Call no man your father" in Matthew 23:9 and realizing that priests are called "Father." The real reason is "I was desperately lonely, and this Evangelical coworker invited me to his church. They welcomed me, gave me a place, knew my name, and loved me."

But Catholics can be welcoming and warm. We too have the ability to open our homes, to invite new folks in the parish over for tea or Sunday dinner. We too can notice gifts and charisms in the lives of newcomers and say, "Hey! You've got a good voice! Have you thought about joining the choir?" or "There's a ladies' prayer meeting. Want to come?"

All this is part of harboring the harborless. Some will complain that this teaches Catholics to look out only "for their own." But this is like complaining that fathers and mothers think first of their children before considering their neighbors. The answer is, "What else do you expect?" Of *course* welcoming the stranger does not stop at our parish doors. But it does start there. And if we cannot welcome the Catholic whom we have seen, how can we welcome the stranger whom we have not seen?

So let us begin where we are, doing what is possible first, before beginning where we are not and doing what is extremely difficult. This is the counsel of the gospel itself, which proceeds not from grand utopian schemes but rather from ordinary people doing what they can where they are—eventually building the temple of God made with living stones, in which all the nations of the earth can find a home.

CHAPTER | 5

Visit the Sick

WE MODERNS CAN BE AWFULLY smug when it comes to Old
Testament taboos. Many people assume such taboos were nothing
but superstitious, prescientific attempts to avoid disease—as though
the Israelites meant to ask, "How do I avoid trichinosis?" but kept
slipping into "How do I keep the cooties away?" All this leads, of
course, to a triumphant conclusion that we are four thousand years
smarter than those people who shackled themselves with barbaric
nonsense about eating unclean food and avoiding people with rashes.
According to this narrative, the great god Progress has freed us from
such ignorant taboos. We now know how to cook pork thoroughly,
what causes leprosy, and how to refrigerate shellfish to avoid
ptomaine. Gleaming science has perfected what Old Testament bar-
barians were groping toward in their ignorance.

This self-congratulatory notion that today we are not motivated by
strictures of ritual impurity is, however, a tad hasty. For the Ick Factor
is as alive and well in our culture as in any other. That's why we are
in no big hurry to brush off some stranger's dandruff, chat up random

women on how their menstrual cycle is going, or touch a corpse. Similarly, before we feel too superior about our coziness with pork and shellfish versus the dietary taboos of ancient Israel, let's ask ourselves how many insect larvae we've eaten lately. Been a while since you've had a yen for brains? Or raw blubber? People in other cultures dine on these perfectly nutritious foods without harm, but we won't touch them. Why? Taboo. The Ick Factor is not confined to ancient Israel.

Scripture, building on this natural human phenomenon, was not establishing a Bronze Age Center for Disease Control. The main focus was on connecting what Israel felt about *biological* ickiness to *spiritual* ickiness. Under inspiration, certain things Israelites found abhorrent—leprosy, effusions of blood, eating pork, touching corpses, and so on—got connected with the repellent nature of sin.

We could pretend that such connections would never ever happen in our vastly more advanced culture. We could pretend that nobody would ever, for instance, attach a moral stigma to AIDS or talk as though a lung-cancer victim had it coming because of the "sin" of smoking. We could pretend that nobody in our culture ever talks as though obesity or addiction to alcohol comes from moral turpitude. We could put on blinkers and pretend nobody today treats the mentally ill as guilty of some special sin instead of as victims of disease.

But the more profitable thing is to admit that humans in every culture have always made connections between physical impurity and moral impurity. The Jews did this too—and so the Old Testament connected their revulsion to leprosy and pork with revulsion toward sin.

In short, God chose to use the image of *pollution*—of some all-soiling, all-pervading contaminant like an infectious agent, or leprosy, or sewage-stained water—to portray what sin is and what it does. And when you think about it, it's an apt image, because sin is not something we can keep to ourselves. It inevitably gets out, like the Ebola virus, and wreaks havoc with the whole of human society. It defiles, infects, poisons, spreads, rots, ruins, and kills.

The problem is that many people learned the wrong lesson from this. Rather than seeing disease as an *image* of sin, not a few (including the apostles) were tempted to see sickness as proof of punishment for sin. Like Job's comforters, many are all too certain that sickness equals divine punishment. Jesus would have none of such simplemindedness. When the disciples asked, "Rabbi, who sinned, this man or his parents, that he was born blind?" Jesus retorted, "It was not that this man sinned, or his parents, but that the works of God might be made manifest in him" (John 9:2, 3).

So Jesus, while using sickness and defilement as an image of sin, did not conflate the image with the reality. Just as he taught that sickness does not mean the victim is a sinner, so he rejected the notion that ritual defilement under the Old Testament means moral defilement:

> "Hear me, all of you, and understand: there is nothing outside a man which by going into him can defile him; but the things which come out of a man are what defile him.". . . And he said to them, "Then are you also without understanding? Do you not see that whatever goes into a man from outside cannot defile him, since it enters, not his heart

but his stomach, and so passes on?" (Thus he declared all foods clean.) And he said, "What comes out of a man is what defiles a man. For from within, out of the heart of man, come evil thoughts, fornication, theft, murder, adultery, coveting, wickedness, deceit, licentiousness, envy, slander, pride, foolishness. All these evil things come from within, and they defile a man." (Mark 7:14–15, 18–23)

His point was that God had taken this natural impulse to regard certain things as defiling and, as with many other natural things, raised it by grace to teach a spiritual lesson. The image of food too gross to eat and things too disgusting to touch was and is an apt image of sin, which sickens the soul as much as pork sickened Jewish stomachs. But Jesus also starkly instructed his followers that it was not food that defiled but sin—that disease was an image of sin, not evidence of the sinfulness of the victim.

Similarly, Jesus had no truck with the pharisaic assumption that saw quarantine as the only possible approach to defilement, whether physical or spiritual. The very name *Pharisee* means "separated one," and Jesus' repudiation of all that is no small part of why he was so hated by them.

Note, for instance, how Jesus insistently went out of his way to associate with the ritually impure. He reached out and touched a leper, committing an act that, under the old law, should have rendered him unclean. But instead Jesus cleansed the leper. That act summarized the new covenant in a nutshell. We see the same message repeated over and over. What renders you unclean under the old covenant is instead made clean by the Messiah of the new. Jesus therefore consorted with gentiles, touched bleeding women and corpses, and (notably for the author of that particular Gospel) welcomed the company of a tax collector named Levi or Matthew (see Matthew 8–10.) The thread that binds all these incidents together is the power of the Spirit to make clean what was unclean. The pharisaic quarantine against defilement is broken.

This conviction that Christ makes clean what was unclean animates the Christian tradition and urges on us the duty to visit the sick. This conviction also links, in the Catholic tradition, two sacraments in particular as the "sacraments of healing": reconciliation and anointing of the sick. The connection is already present, of course, in the words of our Lord: "Those who are well have no need of a physician, but those who are sick," he said, noting that he had come to call not the righteous but sinners to repentance (Mark 2:17).

Once again the image of sickness of body and sickness of soul were linked, but once again sickness was not *identified* with sinfulness. Similarly, in each of these sacraments the relationship of sin and sickness is noted, yet the Church also does not make the mistake of conflating them, as though sickness were a surefire proof of God's wrath. That's why there is a distinction between the sacraments— reconciliation for the sinner, anointing for the sick—yet the sacrament of anointing, while certainly directed at physical healing, is also intended primarily for spiritual healing.

It should be noted that, beyond the sacramental life of the Church, what the tradition commends as a work of mercy is *visiting* the sick, not curing the sick. The goal was not the development of the science of medicine (though that became a happy side effect as the Christian tradition invented the hospital system and encouraged the growth of the sciences). Rather, visiting the sick brings the human dignity of the sufferer into view. Being around illness means being around vomit, pus, running sores, blood, stool, mucus, ghastly injuries, tears, misery, fear, anger, pain, and death. All the corporal work of mercy asks of us, at its most basic, is to screw our courage to the sticking point and have the guts to enter a room, sit down, and hold somebody's fevered hand. And even that is often more than we can muster.

There are, of course, good reasons for that, especially if we happen to live in a time of plague when nobody knows what causes a disease. Part of the reason the Black Death broke the back of medieval Europe is that it decimated the very classes of people (doctors, priests, and other educated people) who lived out this corporal work of mercy—and thus contracted the plague. It takes real courage—and often a strong stomach—to visit the sick.

It can also require moral courage. The Veronica legend reminds us of the stigma that can attach to those who reach out to sufferers. Veronica had the face of the sufferer impressed on her cloth—and her soul—forever. No small part of that is because she had the raw courage to stick out of the crowd. While everybody else either watched Jesus stumble by or, worse still, joined in screaming at him that he would be better off dead (a sentiment as contemporary as our euthanasia culture), Veronica was moved to do this small yet immense act of kindness for the sufferer. She thereby became emblematic of the courage to visit those who suffer not only from bodily illness but from moral disease as well. Veronica had not the slightest idea who this condemned criminal was. He was just part of the rabble Rome had sentenced to die. To judge from the screaming crowd, he might have been a very bad man indeed. Yet she saw his bloody face—and he gave her that face to remember forever. In that moment she became the mother of every saint willing to visit the sick and the sinner, embracing the defilement that conventionality shuns.

Here is one such saint, Catherine of Siena, writing of her care for the condemned criminal Nicolo di Toldo, who asked her to be with him at his execution and whose death she describes:

> I have just taken a head into my hands and have been moved so deeply that my heart cannot grasp it.... I waited for him at the place of execution.... He arrived like a meek lamb and when he saw me he began to smile. He asked me to make the sign of the cross over him.... I stretched out his neck and bent down to him, reminding him of the blood of the Lamb. His lips kept murmuring only "Jesus" and "Catherine," and he was still murmuring when I received his head into my hands.... My soul rested in peace and quiet, so aware of the fragrance of blood that I could not remove the blood which had splashed onto me.[1]

The urging of our Lord to visit the sick is, at bottom, the insistence that we *see* the sick—including those suffering from the sickness called sin—as Catherine of Siena did. It is the call to put faces to names, to honor their human dignity. Instead of calling them "the appendectomy in Room 8" or "that loser that everybody hates" or "that burden on society," we are to call them by their proper names and look them in the eye. The statistical bent of our culture is against this. In our culture without mercy, much can be excused but nothing can be forgiven. So sinners are to be thrown away, not redeemed. As Malcolm Muggeridge observed, to say that God cares more for the one lost sheep than for the ninety and nine who are not lost is "an anti-statistical proposition."[2]

In a cash-strapped culture full of aging baby boomers who are only going to cost more as they age and sicken, this will soon be a subversive and anti-American remark. For as we deal with the morally sick mercilessly, so we shall soon deal with the physically sick and especially the aged. What else can we expect from a culture that kills a million and a half perfectly healthy babies every year for their sin of being inconvenient?

The push, which is already well under way, is not to visit the sick but to hurry them on to the grave, lest they destroy what is left of our economy with their selfish desire to not be murdered by efficient cost-cutting bean counters. Christians who oppose this will soon find themselves the subject of intense legal pressure to play ball and kill off the expensive and used-up geezers, just as they already find themselves the subject of intense pressure to play ball and kill the unborn. When that day arrives, we may again find an appreciation for a Veronican spirituality that looks at the face of the sufferer instead of turning away and babbling happy talk about how he or she will be better off dead. Or we may cave to the culture. Our choice. But whatever we choose, we will still, sooner or later, face the verdict of the King who teaches (and warns) that whatever we do to the least of these, we do to him.

CHAPTER 6

Ransom the Captive

*I*T'S BEEN A WHILE SINCE the Crusades. As a general rule, when our president goes abroad, he does not get waylaid and find himself in the hands of brigands who send back to the vice president wax-sealed notes saying, "Give us forty thousand ducats and we will release your dread sovereign, that he may return to his people amid much rejoicing."

That's not to say kidnappings and ransom demands are unheard of in the modern world. They are, alas, all too common. But one of the differences between the modern and the premodern world is that we don't tend to think of ransoming the captive as a work of mercy. We tend to think of it as a sign of weakness. These days our standard reply to those who demand ransom is, "We do not negotiate with terrorists!"

The idea of ransoming somebody as a *virtue* is an almost completely premodern notion. It depends on two conditions: (1) a society built on slavery (and therefore the taking of slaves), and (2) a not very centralized state that is spotty in its ability to keep people from being enslaved. Under those conditions of frontier semi-justice, the guy who will buy your brother out of captivity after a bandit raid or a skirmish with Saracens when the king and the nobles have no power to do it is a guy you are going to lionize. But since slavery is (thank God) dead in the Western world (due, in the end, to the influence of Christianity) and cops are now the ones who deal with hostage situations, we no longer have a living experience of how ransoming might be virtuous.

Our principal encounters with ransoming the captive as a virtuous work of mercy tend to come via historical dramas like *Les Misérables*. The kindly bishop, on finding Jean Valjean in custody for stealing the clergyman's silver, insists to the gendarmes that the silver was a gift rather than stolen—and that Valjean must take the candlesticks as well. Having thus set him free, the bishop tells him, "Jean Valjean, my brother, you no longer belong to evil, but to good. It is your soul that I buy from you; I withdraw it from black thoughts and the spirit of perdition, and I give it to God."[1]

Beautiful and moving. But how do we live this precept out in this day and age?

One way is to support agencies such as Anti-Slavery International, which exist to remind us that just because slavery has been largely banished in Christian lands doesn't mean it's banished everywhere. In fact, at this hour, slavery is a thriving concern in many parts of the world. It is also, in all but name, supported by global corporations that outsource to countries where they can turn a fatter profit by paying sweatshop drudges bare subsistence pennies instead of dollars. Child slaves, sex slaves, slaves of all ages and of a multiplicity of nationalities toil across the globe at this hour.

Of course, there is always a spiritual application to these things as well. Thus Jesus announced his own ministry by proclaiming the words of Isaiah:

> The Spirit of the Lord is upon me, / because he has anointed me to preach good news to the poor. / He has sent me to *proclaim release to the captives* / and recovering of sight to the blind, / to *set at liberty those who are oppressed,* / to proclaim the acceptable year of the Lord. (Luke 4:18–19, emphasis mine)

And yet, in the political sense, Jesus set no captives free, liberated no oppressed people. He led no storming of the Bastille, no Underground Railroad, no ransom of King Richard Lionheart. So how did our Lord fulfill this prophecy?

Jesus gave us several hints. For instance, he exorcised and healed the demoniac who, "kept under guard, and bound with chains and shackles, . . . broke the bonds and was driven by the demon into the desert" (Luke 8:26–39). The man had been "liberated" in the merely physical sense when Jesus found him. And yet the iron chains he broke are nothing compared to the spiritual chains Jesus broke for him. Likewise, the woman with the infirmity (Luke 13:10–17) was described by Jesus as "bound" (v. 16), and her healing foreshadows the complete healing of body, soul, and spirit he means for us.

So not surprisingly, the way Jesus described his mission was precisely in terms of slavery and ransom for the captive. It is worth quoting the passage in full, for it reveals how radical Jesus' approach to the issues of power and slavery were:

And James and John, the sons of Zebedee, came forward to him, and said to him, "Teacher, we want you to do for us whatever we ask of you." And he said to them, "What do you want me to do for you?" And they said to him, "Grant us to sit, one at your right hand and one at your left, in your glory." But Jesus said to them, "You do not know what you are asking. Are you able to drink the chalice that I drink, or to be baptized with the baptism with which I am baptized?" And they said to him, "We are able." And Jesus said to them, "The chalice that I drink you will drink; and with the baptism with which I am baptized, you will be baptized; but to sit at my right hand or at my left is not mine to grant, but it is for those for whom it has been prepared." And when the ten heard it, they began to be indignant at James and John. And Jesus called them to him and said to them, "You know that those who are supposed to rule over the Gentiles lord it over them, and their great men exercise authority over them. But it shall not be so among you; but whoever would be great among you must be your servant, and whoever would be first among you must be slave of all. For the Son of man also came not to be served but to serve, and to give his life as a ransom for many." (Mark 10:35–45)

Note the big picture here. James and John were seeking to sit at Jesus' right and left because they believed this new Son of David was much like the old son of David, Solomon. What had Solomon done? He had built a splendid kingdom—on the backs of slaves. That's what oriental potentates did. That's why Solomon was remembered with a mixture of pride and resentment in the Old Testament. On the one hand, his reign was a golden age of immense national pride. On the other hand, he became a new pharaoh in order to achieve these goals. When his son Rehoboam promised to continue his policies, the news was greeted not with excitement but with civil war and the permanent loss of ten tribes of Israel (see 1 Kings 12).

Now someone greater than Solomon was here, and James and John were all about getting in on the action as top dogs over a new kingdom of slaves doing their bidding. It was that ambition that Jesus rebuked with his new definition of greatness. And what a new definition it is! He proposed not merely to ransom the captive with money or gold as a king like Solomon might have done. He proposed to ransom the captive by *taking the captive's place as a slave!*

For as he made clear, the ultimate form of slavery is spiritual, and the whole world lies in the power of the evil one (see 1 John 5:19):

> Jesus then said to the Jews who had believed in him, "If you continue in my word, you are truly my disciples, and you will know the truth, and the truth will make you free." They answered him, "We are descendants of Abraham, and have never been in bondage to any one. How is it that you say, 'You will be made free'?"
>
> Jesus answered them, "Truly, truly, I say to you, every one who commits sin is a slave to sin. The slave does not continue in the house for ever; the son continues for ever. So if the Son makes you free, you will be free indeed." (John 8:31–36)

Slavery to sin, with its various spin-off forms such as slavery to addiction, fear, violence, and so forth, is the root of all the slavery in the world. Attack that and you ultimately attack physical forms of slavery.

That's why one of the craziest complaints about the Christian revelation is that it is somehow responsible for the existence of slavery. In fact, it's the only thing that, in the long run, ever expunged the cursed thing from the face of the earth. To complain that it happened in the long run rather than instantly is like complaining that an Olympic weight lifter took a long time to stoop down, get a firm grip on the bar, summon his might, and then hoist the three thousand pounds over his head. Slavery has been absolutely endemic everywhere in the human race since the dawn of time. The one and only thing that *ever* succeeded in beating it back and rooting it out is the Christian tradition. That it took a long time and a lot of back-and-forth struggle to do it is due not to some peculiar and disgusting weakness in the Christian tradition but rather to the fact that the Christian revelation was born into a world of mortals who took slavery for granted as the normal state of things, just as we take all our favorite sins as normal and resent having them challenged. The reaction of the Jews in the passage above—the Jews *who had believed in him*, mind you, not the Jews who rejected him—is our reaction: "Whaddaya mean, calling *us* slaves?" Our culture's conception of freedom is "doing whatever I feel like." Usually that means "doing what everybody else does." In antiquity "everybody else" lived in a slave culture.

Meanwhile, in our culture we continue to live with a false conception of slavery and freedom. We have no notion that "doing whatever we feel like" is often a straight road into bondage. Addicts to drugs, alcohol, violence, pornography, and sloth all "do what they feel like." Indeed, we may be quite decent citizens who pay our taxes and recycle, all while living in slavery to raw, unadulterated pride—the sin that made the devil the devil. Confronted with a real saint who is a slave to Christ (and therefore truly free), we may find that our conversation with him goes uncomfortably like the conversation between the ghost and the heavenly spirit in C.S. Lewis's *The Great Divorce*. The ghost, after boasting about what a decent chap he is, says, "I'm only telling you the sort of chap I am. I only want my rights. I'm not asking for anybody's bleeding charity." To which the blessed spirit of his old comrade replies, "Then do. At once. Ask for the Bleeding Charity. Everything is here for the asking and nothing can be bought."[2]

In short, the first captive you can involve yourself in ransoming is yourself, sold as a slave to sin. Or more precisely, you can submit to the ransom already offered when, for your sake, Jesus Christ was sold as a slave for thirty pieces of silver and, with that silver, said, "My brother, you no longer belong to evil but to good. It is your soul that I buy from you; I withdraw it from black thoughts and the spirit of perdition, and I give it to God." This hostage exchange is made every time someone is baptized, or goes to confession, or celebrates the Eucharist or one of the other sacraments.

Once you have accepted that ransom, pay it forward as best you can by telling somebody else about the great ransom. Then you will be well on the way to living that work of mercy in the highest sense of the word.

Bury the Dead

"*T*HE BODY," I WAS TAUGHT growing up, "is just the shoe box for the soul. What matters are the shoes, not the box. So when it's time to go to heaven, we throw the box away."

Along with this good solid dose of gnostic thinking came a certain aesthetic that regarded the human person as a ghost in a machine. Of course, I didn't *live* as though I was a ghost in a machine. Nobody does, except perhaps a victim of extreme mental illness. Practically speaking, I lived as you do: in the instinctive awareness that I am a unity of body and soul. That's why when Susie stuck out her tongue at me when I was four, I knew that her soul was, in union with her body, expressing the thought that I was yucky. And when I cried as a result, it was not the tear ducts of my bio-envelope that were sad. It was me—the union of body and soul—that felt rejected.

None of that changed as I grew up. When I was nine, I wrote my name all over my older brother's TV screen with an eraser. Mike would not have been persuaded of my innocence had I been precocious enough to exclaim, "Do not take out your wrath on my bottom by spanking me in a fury, for the actions of the body are disconnected from the purity of the soul!" Nor, indeed, was my brother's firm bottom-swatting something my soul quickly forgot.

Still and all, despite the constant reminder of experience, gnosticism remains one of the most perennially popular forms of nonsense. Gnostics think like Yoda: "Luminous beings are we, not this crude matter." They assume that the way to figure out what constitutes a human being is to saw the person into two components: worthless body and valuable soul. This notion has infected Christian thought like a virus since the birth of the Church—and it still wreaks havoc today.

So, for instance, some people attempt moral reasoning about abortion by asking questions like "What's the difference between human life and human tissue?" Beneath that question lurks the idea: "The spirit of Joe Smith is what makes him a person. The valueless bag of genetic chemicals that is the body of Joe Smith is just the shoe box. When we separate the one from the other, we'll know when Joe Smith comes into existence and when it is OK to abort him or manipulate those chemicals in a lab."

The problem is, no part of the created order is valueless. Rather, God calls all creation "good" (see Genesis 1) and, as St. Thomas Aquinas observed, God's grace (the grace that brings every baby into existence) perfects nature rather than destroying, supplanting, or ignoring it.

Grace creates a hierarchy of goodness in which each created thing remains itself while becoming part of something greater than itself. So in the creation of every human being, God raises atoms to participate in molecular existence, yet atoms remain atoms. Likewise, molecules are raised to participate in organic chemistry yet remain molecules. And so on with organic chemicals, DNA, single-celled and multicellular organisms. Each is, by the power of God, raised to participate in something higher, yet each thing remains what it is. And at the pinnacle of the hierarchy, one multicellular species is raised by grace to participate not merely in a new level of natural life but in the supernatural life of God himself. Thus, humans are animals with a rational soul in the image and likeness of God (see Genesis 1:27, 2:7). Yet we're not thereby "spiritualized" out of our bodies and into the ether. Rather, we retain our hair, fangs, claws, and DNA. So we are, to be sure, dust. But this dust *is*—not merely "contains"—a person.

This is not to say it's impossible to separate soul and body. Indeed, it happens thousands of times every day. It's called "death." And death is precisely the bitter fruit of the fall from which Christ saves us. Thus the sought-for separation of soul and body can *never* show us the beginning of human life, only its end—leaving only a corpse and a ghost. In a grim way, even sin and death show the essential unity of flesh and spirit.

The real way to approach the question is sacramentally, by asking, "What is the *relationship*, not the difference, between body, soul, and spirit?" Christianity tells us that human soul and body are related not as milk to milk bottle but as *Mona Lisa* to paint. Human beings are not souls poured into disposable, finely tuned bags of genetic chemicals. We are, as Scripture says, an inseparable unity of body, soul, and spirit (see Genesis 2:7; 1 Thessalonians 5:23). And if you want to know when a human being begins life, ask yourself, "At what moment did the Son of God become the Son of Man, the paradigm of the human race?" The answer of two thousand years of unbroken Catholic tradition is plain: In the supreme instance of his identification with the human person—by the life-giving power that loved creation into being, blessed the hierarchy of goodness, and came to save the world from sin and death—God the Son of Man was *conceived by the Holy Spirit* (see Matthew 1:20; Luke 1:35).

The Incarnation of the Son of God is why the Christian tradition has always hallowed the body, not only in life but even in death. For the body does not derive its holiness, significance, and worth simply from being associated with a soul. It derives it from God, who made the body as the temple not only of the human soul but of the living God himself. It is sacred in death, even as the ruins of the temple in Jerusalem and the dead body of Jesus were sacred. For in the Risen Christ that body shall be rebuilt.

This sanctity of the body is something that has been intuited since the very dawn of humanity. With the appearance of humankind we see the very first occurrence of something that does not occur in all the billions of years of life on earth before us: the grave. Suddenly we find not merely animal carcasses strewn on the ground but the bodies of *persons* laid with reverence in the ground, buried with flowers, entombed with tokens of things they loved in life, decked with art that speaks of some groping hope that this is not the end for them, surrounded with the love, respect, or awe their fellows had for them.

The ambiguity of our position as fallen creatures is on full display in how we treat the dead. In the Old Testament, burying the dead is as much a pious work of mercy as it is in the Christian tradition. But as in the Christian tradition, it is also something nobody is especially eager to do. Under the old covenant, touching the dead, for instance, rendered a person ritually unclean, just as today it can traumatize you, make you sick, or give you the creeps. There's a reason every civilization and culture in the world has ghost stories and feels the dead to be uncanny. We sense in our bones that the division of body and soul is *wrong*. We feel the absence of the one who should be there. And we are none too eager to look on the face of the dead.

And yet, burying the dead remains a work of mercy. For Christians the archetype of this work was seen in the deposition from the cross and in the women's later coming to the tomb to anoint Jesus' body. Indeed, so significant is the work of caring for and burying the dead that one woman in particular will be remembered for this act down to the end of time:

> And while he was at Bethany in the house of Simon the leper, as he sat at table, a woman came with an alabaster jar of ointment of pure nard, very costly, and she broke the jar and poured it over his head. But there were some who said to themselves indignantly, "Why was the ointment thus wasted? For this ointment might have been sold for more than three hundred denarii, and given to the poor." And they reproached her. But Jesus said, "Let her alone; why do you trouble her? She has done a beautiful thing to me. For you always have the poor with you, and whenever you will, you can do good to them; but you will not always have me. She has done what she could; she has anointed my body before-

hand for burying. And truly, I say to you, wherever the gospel is preached in the whole world, what she has done will be told in memory of her." (Mark 14:3–9)

The utilitarian approach to the dead and those doomed to die that is exemplified by Mary's critics is still very much with us—and is growing as the euthanasia movement grows, urging the weak and inconvenient to die and get out of the way, while simultaneously promising us a secular utopia through war and the raw exercise of earthly power. Sometimes it can reveal itself with a white-hot hatred of the weak and those who care for them.

Exhibit A: Mother Teresa founds a home in Calcutta specifically ordered toward honoring those who cannot be saved from death. In doing so, she blasphemes against a central tenet of post-Christian faith in progress: the doctrine that we shall sooner or later conquer death itself. She reminds us, by her Home for the Dying, that we are all going to end up there sooner or later and that sometimes what is necessary is to reverence the dying by giving them their true human dignity. This is, in fact, a million miles away from what our culture of death calls "death with dignity," for Mother Teresa does not murder the dying with poison or blather about weeding out the unfit to make room for the productive. Instead she simply honors the dying, cares for their bodily needs, and prays for them as they leave this world.

The response of atheist Trotskyite Christopher Hitchens to her? "I wish there was a hell for the bitch to go to."[1] To embrace our holy sister, the death of the body, enrages the children of this world now no less than it enraged Judas then.

For death is the last impregnable fortress against our pride; the last reminder that sin cannot win, that our power is not eternal, that God is not mocked. It is also, by the grace of that same God, no longer a hole but a door. Our salvation has been won precisely through the death of the one whose body Mary of Bethany anointed. It was that dead body, and no other, that was raised from death in glory and that is now the means by which God mediates his eternal life to us in the sacrament of Jesus' Body and Blood.

The body of our beloved dead is, therefore, like Jesus' body, both a memorial and a pledge of future salvation. It is the last relic we have of our beloved—and the seed of the person's resurrection. So we honor it even in death. As Paul says:

> What you sow does not come to life unless it dies. And what you sow is not the body which is to be, but a bare kernel, perhaps of wheat or of some other grain. But God gives it a body as he has chosen, and to each kind of seed its own body. For not all flesh is alike, but there is one kind for men, another for animals, another for birds, and another for fish. There are celestial bodies and there are terrestrial bodies; but the glory of the celestial is one, and the glory of the terrestrial is another. There is one glory of the sun, and another glory of the moon, and another glory of the stars; for star differs from star in glory.
>
> So is it with the resurrection of the dead. What is sown is perishable, what is raised is imperishable. It is sown in dishonor, it is raised in glory. It is sown in weakness, it is raised in power. It is sown a physical body, it is raised a spiritual

body. If there is a physical body, there is also a spiritual body. Thus it is written, "The first man Adam became a living soul"; the last Adam became a life-giving spirit. But it is not the spiritual which is first but the physical, and then the spiritual. The first man was from the earth, a man of dust; the second man is from heaven. As was the man of dust, so are those who are of the dust; and as is the man of heaven, so are those who are of heaven. Just as we have borne the image of the man of dust, we shall also bear the image of the man of heaven. I tell you this, brethren: flesh and blood cannot inherit the kingdom of God, nor does the perishable inherit the imperishable.

Lo! I tell you a mystery. We shall not all sleep, but we shall all be changed, in a moment, in the twinkling of an eye, at the last trumpet. For the trumpet will sound, and the dead will be raised imperishable, and we shall be changed. For this perishable nature must put on the imperishable, and this mortal nature must put on immortality. When the perishable puts on the imperishable, and the mortal puts on immortality, then shall come to pass the saying that is written:

Death is swallowed up in victory.
O death, where is your victory?
O death, where is your sting?"
(1 Corinthians 15:54–55)

CHAPTER | 8

Instruct the Ignorant

BACK IN 1971, WHEN EXPERIMENTS in educational theory were all the rage, my fellow seventh-graders and I were pulled out of what used to be called a "junior high" and packed off to a newly built experiment in education called Eisenhower Middle School. It was the latest thing: a school without walls, a great wheel-shaped building comprising various "learning areas," where education would miraculously unfold as the natural instinct for learning that swells in the breast of every child was watered and nourished by a whole panoply of audiovisual materials, media resources, and the free exchange of ideas among the different-aged children. The idea was that, left to ourselves, we young skulls full of mush naturally ached to unlock the mysteries of the Stamp Act, the Hanseatic League, pre-algebra, and sentence diagramming.

It turned out we didn't even want to read *Lord of the Flies*, which our experiment in learning soon came to resemble. We ate weary teachers alive. We found the verdant wood surrounding the school grounds an excellent hideout for skipping class and learning to smoke. I strongly suspect we brought on the early death (from sheer exhaustion and frustration) of at least one of our aging math teachers. We wasted lots of time making "video productions" that basically consisted of shooting each other making faces. Undoubtedly there were some students out at the end of the bell curve who, like Lisa Simpson, wanted to slake their burning thirst for knowledge. But for most of us, given the choice between actual education and what the young folk today call "hanging out with our friends," the choice was easy: Cracking jokes with your buddies about how stupid everybody (especially your teacher) was turned out to be highly preferable to studying things we didn't know about. Ignorance truly was bliss.

This experience more or less sums up the problem facing anybody who attempts to live out the first of the spiritual works of mercy, instructing the ignorant. For it turns out that ignorance and arrogance are virtually always twins. The less you know, the more likely you are to be cocky about it. And so C.S. Lewis remarks that the main task in attempting the project of education is not cutting down jungles but irrigating deserts. The person who really knows what he or she is talking about, who has seen a bit of the world and knows (either by personal experience or by a deep and appreciative reading) something of the beauties and horrors it offers—such can be stymied by the sheer bullish indifference of the ignoramus brimming with the insolence of youth. It can be a trial to coax such cold indifference out of its cramped world of video games and comic books to feel the slightest spark of interest in the heartbreaking vision of Pickett's troops marching straight into a Union fusillade at Gettysburg, or the structure of reality that fascinated Einstein, or the musical architecture of Bach, or the compact brilliance of Dante, or the bottomless genius of Shakespeare—or the densely layered revelations of Scripture.

This correlation between ignorance and arrogance did not, of course, arise merely with that peculiarly arrogant form of ignorance called modern atheism. The curse of ignorance predates the modern ripple of atheism by centuries, and no culture or religious tradition has been exempt from it. It was into a deeply religious world that Christianity was born, and it was this world that Christ instructed. Humanly speaking, he did not inaugurate the practice of instructing the ignorant (though, of course, his Holy Spirit has been behind the whole project from the start). Again and again the Hebrew Scriptures called Israel to, as we moderns say, "get a clue." Moses made it simple: Obedience to God's law brings good results, and disobedience brings bad ones:

> For this commandment which I command you this day is not too hard for you, neither is it far off. It is not in heaven, that you should say, "Who will go up for us to heaven, and bring it to us, that we may hear it and do it?" Neither is it beyond the sea, that you should say, "Who will go over the sea for us, and bring it to us, that we may hear it and do it?" But the word is very near you; it is in your mouth and in your heart, so that you can do it.
>
> See, I have set before you this day life and good, death and evil. If you obey the commandments of the LORD your God which I command you this day, by loving the LORD your

God, by walking in his ways, and by keeping his commandments and his statutes and his ordinances, then you shall live
and multiply, and the LORD your God will bless you in the
land which you are entering to take possession of it. But if
your heart turns away, and you will not hear, but are drawn
away to worship other gods and serve them, I declare to you
this day, that you shall perish; you shall not live long in the
land which you are going over the Jordan to enter and possess. I call heaven and earth to witness against you this day,
that I have set before you life and death, blessing and curse;
therefore choose life, that you and your descendants may
live, loving the LORD your God, obeying his voice, and
clinging to him; for that means life to you and length of
days, that you may dwell in the land which the LORD swore
to your fathers, to Abraham, to Isaac, and to Jacob, to give
them. (Deuteronomy 30:11–20)

This habit of the Hebraic tradition to append very clear threats and
promises to the terms of the covenant irritates sophisticated moderns. But it's not really such a riddle. As Flannery O'Connor pointed
out, "To the hard of hearing, you shout." So the prophets continually
shout to Israel (and to us) that "the fear of the LORD is the beginning
of wisdom" (Proverbs 9:10), because Old Testament Israel was, as her
history attests, deaf with the deafness of the mule-headed—the most
profound kind of deafness. So Isaiah must open his great book with
the cry of frustration:

Hear, O heavens, and give ear, O earth; / for the LORD has
spoken:

"Sons have I reared and brought up, / but they have rebelled against me. / The ox knows its owner, / and the ass its master's crib; / but Israel does not know, / my people does not understand." (Isaiah 1:2–3)

(This cry, by the way, is echoed in the tradition of Christian nativity iconography. There is always an ox and an ass pictured in the stable because the "welcome" given to Christ on his arrival on earth is foreshadowed in this passage—and still lived out today in our failure to welcome the poor.)

Isaiah's pedagogy of the ignorant was emphatically directed at a people who were ignorant not because of lack of information but because of a willed and deliberate *choice* to be ignorant:

To whom then will you liken God, / or what likeness compare with him? / The idol! a workman casts it, / and a goldsmith overlays it with gold, / and casts for it silver chains. / He who is impoverished chooses for an offering / wood that will not rot; / he seeks out a skilful craftsman / to set up an image that will not move. / Have you not known? Have you not heard? / Has it not been told you from the beginning? / Have you not understood from the foundations of the earth? (Isaiah 40:18–21)

Indeed, one of the marks of the prophets was their curious note of gentleness toward the gentiles, who, while often unbelievably brutal and blind, were cut more slack than Israel because their ignorance was due precisely to the fact that they had not enjoyed Israel's privileges. As Paul noted:

First Moses says, / "I will make you jealous of those who are not a nation; / with a foolish nation I will make you angry." / Then Isaiah is so bold as to say, / "I have been found by those who did not seek me; / I have shown myself to those who did not ask for me." / But of Israel he says, "All day long I have held out my hands to a disobedient and contrary people." (Romans 10:19–21)

Some people are inclined to read this as though Paul were sucking up to the gentiles and kicking Israel down the stairs. On the contrary, for Paul, Israel was the custodian of the "oracles of God" (Romans 3:2), while the gentile pagans lived in stygian darkness. Following Jesus, Paul thought that "every one to whom much is given, of him will much be required" (Luke 12:48). Not only should Israel have known better; she should have been a light to the gentiles. Instead she failed more seriously than the gentiles, by rejecting her own Messiah. So God, in his wisdom, would make the foolish gentiles the provocation for Israel to return to God. For Paul, the truth was that, in Christ, each depends on all. So while Israel was instructed and provoked to faith in Christ by the conversion of the gentiles, the gentiles received their instruction for their salvation from the oracles of Israel as fulfilled in Christ. As Isaiah says:

Arise, shine; for your light has come, / and the glory of the LORD has risen upon you. / For behold, darkness shall cover the earth, / and thick darkness the peoples; / but the LORD will arise upon you, /and his glory will be seen upon you. / And nations shall walk by your light, / and kings in the brightness of your rising. (Isaiah 60:1–3)

The notion that Jew or gentile can claim to be top dog in the pedagogy of salvation is like the idea of patients in a cancer ward squabbling about who is the least terminal. Our position, under God, is that "all have sinned and fall short of the glory of God" (Romans 3:23). And that's the problem when it comes to instructing the ignorant. For just as the ignorant can be proud of their ignorance, so the learned can be even prouder of their learning. Indeed, that was the problem that had come to poison Israel's relationship with the gentiles. As Paul put it:

> But if you call yourself a Jew and rely upon the law and boast of your relation to God and know his will and approve what is excellent, because you are instructed in the law, and if you are sure that you are a guide to the blind, a light to those who are in darkness, a corrector of the foolish, a teacher of children, having in the law the embodiment of knowledge and truth—you then who teach others, will you not teach yourself? While you preach against stealing, do you steal? You who say that one must not commit adultery, do you commit adultery? You who abhor idols, do you rob temples? You who boast in the law, do you dishonor God by breaking the law? For, as it is written, "The name of God is blasphemed among the Gentiles because of you." (Romans 2:17–24)

In short, the problem facing us in instructing the ignorant is not the arrogant ignoramus versus the virtuous teacher. It is the arrogant ignoramus versus the arrogant teacher. And the teacher's arrogance can be even more deeply sinful than that of the ignoramus, because he ought to know better. That's why Jesus, like the prophets, has more words of rebuke for the prideful scribes and teachers of the law than he has for the gentiles who worship stars or rocks. Indeed, Jesus warned strongly against this temptation, going so far as to say:

> The scribes and the Pharisees sit on Moses' seat; so practice and observe whatever they tell you, but not what they do; for they preach, but do not practice. They bind heavy burdens, hard to bear, and lay them on men's shoulders; but they themselves will not move them with their finger. They do all their deeds to be seen by men; for they make their phylacteries broad and their fringes long, and they love the place of honor at feasts and the best seats in the synagogues, and salutations in the market places, and being called rabbi by men. But you are not to be called rabbi, for you have one teacher, and you are all brethren. And call no man your father on earth, for you have one Father, who is in heaven. Neither be called masters, for you have one master, the Christ. He who is greatest among you shall be your servant; whoever exalts himself will be humbled, and whoever humbles himself will be exalted. (Matthew 23:2–12)

These words are not to be read in a literalist fashion, any more than the command to "call no man your father on earth" means that sending your dad a Father's Day card is a sin. Jesus' point is not to erect some absurd taboo against calling people "teacher." We can know this because Paul specifically tells us that God's "gifts were that some should be apostles, some prophets, some evangelists, some pastors and teachers, to equip the saints for the work of ministry, for building up the body of Christ" (Ephesians 4:11–12).

Rather, Jesus means we cannot imagine that our knowledge of some particular field—and above all, our knowledge of the revelation entrusted to the Church—is our property or the fruit of our genius or personal sanctity. We are forbidden to see our knowledge as a sign of our spiritual superiority. As Paul says, "Knowledge puffs up, but love builds up" (1 Corinthians 8:1).

So knowledge in the service of love, not pride, is the goal of instructing the ignorant. This is a work that is demanded of all of us sooner or later. The world groans for those with competence in an area of knowledge to impart that knowledge to those who lack it. That's because humans are not insects or horses, born with enough knowledge to take care of themselves within seconds or hours. Beyond the swallow reflex, virtually every human activity is taught us by somebody, and we are therefore all raised as debtors to a civilization we shall never be able to repay. Each of us has had a thousand teachers, not merely at school but from myriad other backgrounds and vocations. Each of us can point to people who taught us everything we know, who showed us the ropes about our jobs, our passions, our relationships—and about God.

The interesting thing is that, when it comes to the office of teacher (and, in particular, that teacher who is given to us by Christ himself, our bishop), Christ chose to distinguish the holder of that office from those whom we call "saints." Indeed, he seems to have gone out of his way to do so. As Chesterton remarked concerning the establishment of the office that, above all others, is the supreme teaching office in the Church:

When Christ at a symbolic moment was establishing His great society, He chose for its corner-stone neither the brilliant Paul nor the mystic John, but a shuffler, a snob, a coward—in a word, a man. And upon this rock He has built His Church, and the gates of Hell have not prevailed against it. All the empires and the kingdoms have failed, because of this inherent and continual weakness, that they were founded by strong men and upon strong men. But this one thing, the historic Christian Church, was founded on a weak man, and for that reason it is indestructible. For no chain is stronger than its weakest link.[1]

Over the past several years we have heard a massive amount of nonsense spoken in the media about how bishops "lose their moral authority to teach" when it turns out that they are sinners, fools, or failures. But this is not so, for the gospel never derived from their "moral authority" in the first place. Indeed, the choice of Simon Peter for first pope makes it screamingly clear that no bishop derives the gospel from his personal "moral authority." All—and I mean *all*—a bishop does when he teaches is to hand down a body of doctrine that he did not invent, that he cannot subtract from, that he cannot add to—and that does not depend one iota on his personal "moral authority." A *saint* teaches by personal moral authority. A saint's essential teaching is this: "Imitate me as I imitate Christ" (see 1 Corinthians 11:1). People are attracted to his personal charisma and the way he or she embodies the message of Christ. When by happy chance a bishop is also a saint, his sanctity certainly sweetens the message that he transmits. But the truth of that message no more depends on his moral authority than the truth that two plus two equals four depends on the personal holiness of your math teacher. Likewise, as Peter made clear by his rash promise, his cowardly betrayal, his vacillating wimpiness, and his general thickheadedness, the truth of his message did not depend on his personal qualities of heroism.

Paradoxically, this is why the Church has always insisted on the unity of truth and holiness even as she likewise has always warned against predicating our faith in the gospel on the relative sanctity of the episcopal messenger who proclaims it. To be sure, bishops, priests, and lay evangelists *should* be holy. But if they are not, this does not affect the truth of what they say one bit, for the truth is found in Jesus Christ and not in the extremely frail members of his body. The danger of ignoring this warning is quickly seen whenever some factional fanboy arrives on the scene shouting, "I am of Paul! I am of Apollos!"

Different factions in the Church tend to anoint different celebrities as the *real* teachers of the faith, owing to a perception that their heroes are holier and more competent to teach than "the bishops" (the vague plural is essential to such rhetoric). It might be a fave rave apologist. It might be Speaking Truth to Power Peace 'n' Justice guy. It might be Pure and Perfect Liturgy guy. It might be Theology of the Body guy. It might be Angry Nun With a Conscience. It might be some other celebrity popular with half a dozen other little subcultures in the Church who work to trump the teaching of the church with his or her favorite pet theory. But the fact remains, the primary teachers of the faith are (and always will be) the bishops. Hive off after your favorite hero and elevate him or her above the full-orbed teaching of the Church articulated by the magisterium and you will, it is absolutely guaranteed, wind up with a mere fragment of the faith instead of the full-meal deal Jesus intended. In short, you will wind up ignorant, not fully Catholic.

Instructing the ignorant (particularly with respect to the faith) is, like all things pertaining to the faith, risky business. Knowledge puffs up, and knowledge of holy things puffs *way* up. The gratifying thought "Get me! I am instructing the ignorant" can steal in very subtly. Exasperation with those who are proud of their ignorance can be a fine catalyst for pride in one's knowledge, puny though it must always be when it comes to God. But the thing, nonetheless, must be done and can be done with the help of Christ.

For laypeople to whom the task of teaching falls, what must always be held in mind is that we are, at best, merely helpers of the bishops and never their replacements. For the ordained, the grace to teach, sanctify, and govern places them, as our Lord said, in the position of the servant and not the master. And for all of us, the fundamental reality remains that we are—every last one of us—the ignorant whom the Divine Instructor is patiently teaching till the school bell rings on that Day and we enter into the greatest summer vacation of all time.

CHAPTER | 9

Counsel the Doubtful

DOUBT CAN BE THE EMOTIONAL equivalent of a brief spring rain or a hurricane. People doubt whether to place two bucks on the Mariners (don't) or whether the God in whom they have trusted all their life is a sham, fraud, and delusion. Doubt can be a healthy exercise in learning to put aside our tribal prejudices, or it can be a soul-shattering crisis that radically remakes or destroys us.

The difficult thing about counseling the doubtful is that doubt isn't always bad and confidence isn't always good.

For instance, one of the trendy notions afoot is the so-called theology of doubt, whereby a supposed new breed of progressive Christian eschews the "rigid dogmas" of the past and treats Christian tradition with an "open mind." What this almost invariably means is that the new breed of Christian is trading in his parents' set of assumptions for a new set, usually based on whatever ideology or current pop-culture norms his peers accept. So this supposedly open-minded doubter has lots of doubts about the Virgin Birth, the Resurrection, or the proper use of the pelvis. But he has no doubt that condoms promote "safe sex," that divorce and remarriage are no big deal, and that only a churl could feel skepticism about the wisdom of gay marriage.

Such folk think nearly anything they like about Jesus Christ. (Was he eaten by wild dogs, as John Dominic Crossan says?[1] Gay, as Elton John says?[2] The table is open for a freewheeling discussion!) But there is only one way to think about smoking, women's ordination, or anthropogenic global warming.[3]

Similarly, on the reactionary side of the aisle, a reflection of this misplaced doubt and certitude has been emerging. There we often hear that we just can't trust the teaching of the bishops, since the Second Vatican Council allegedly perverted everything. So we must ignore the purportedly heterodox bishops except on one subject and one subject alone.

This mentality can be summarized as "Opposition to abortion and euthanasia taketh away the sins of the world." It is the theory that one is completely free to ignore and even heap contempt on the Church's clear teaching on virtually any subject just so long as one opposes abortion and euthanasia. So whether it be the clear and obvious desire of the Church to abolish the death penalty, the reiterated prohibition of the use of torture, the Church's clear warning that "the concept of a 'preventive war' does not appear in the *Catechism of the Catholic Church*,"[4] the teaching of the Church that health care is a right, or any other matter of public concern, the argument of many reactionaries is that none of these things need be heeded or even treated with respect, just so long as one is opposed to abortion and euthanasia.

In this topsy-turvy world, we are condemned to a universe of doubt about almost every Catholic moral teaching beyond "abortion is wrong." But that's not to say reactionary dissent lacks certitude any more than progressive dissent does. There is often utter certitude about the worthlessness of the Paul VI Mass, the disposability of Paul VI's and John Paul II's teachings, the sinfulness of church architecture or hymnody not to one's taste, or the use of banners in the sanctuary. One can, in such circles, discover infallible proclamations that Harry Potter is evil, that true Catholic parents homeschool, that Mary is most assuredly appearing (or most assuredly *not* appearing) at Medjugorje, and that waterboarding is nothing more than a harmless splash of water.

In short, the problem is often not merely "faith versus doubt." It's that people are doubtful about what the Church says is trustworthy (like the Mass or the social and moral teaching of the Church) and are possessed of adamantine certitude about things that common sense or the Church's magisterium urge us to treat as ambiguous, cheerfully latitudinarian, dubiously quacky, or just plain wrong. In such cases reactionary dissenters, no less than progressive dissenters, often simply tune out the magisterium and common sense and run to their favorite celebrity theologian, visionary, or media talking hairdo to reinforce their certitude about the doubtful thing and their doubt about the solid and obvious thing.

Yet, for all their hostility to one another, the progressive and the reactionary do have one thing in common: the notion that an old-fashioned "pre–Vatican II" faith that is coterminous with rigid ideological certitude is being replaced with a "new" Catholic faith that is riddled with doubt. On both sides of the aisle, the basic story is this: In the pre–Vatican II Church, you knew exactly what was what, which was without nuance, paradox, or ambiguity. This simple world of *Baltimore Catechism* blacks and whites was swept away by the post–Vatican II Church of Ambiguity. Such folk often talk as though they eagerly await (or desperately dread) the day when some Third Vatican Council is called to finish the work of demolition and reconstruction begun by the Second Vatican Council. (Progressive dissenters and reactionary dissenters disagree only on whether that narrative is a happy story or a tragedy.)

In fact, that narrative is not true at all, because there are not two Churches, pre- and postconciliar. There is simply the one, holy, catholic, and apostolic Church. And what that Church has always offered us is *faith*, not certitude or doubt. For the Catholic faith has always been in a God who is a mystery, not a fog, ideology, political platform, diagram, formula, or equation.

How then do we approach the false doubts and false dogmatism of the sundry human factions that always contend within the bosom of the Church? The first thing to do is remember, "'Twas ever thus." Paul had to rebuke factionalists repeatedly. The early Church had party spirit in spades, rioting and battling it out in Ephesus, Constantinople, Rome, and any other place where Christians got excited about anything from politics to soccer.

In short, the faith in its theological teaching (summed up in the creeds and dogmas of the Church) tells us a few certain and definite things about God and the human person, and then it leaves much of the rest of life for us to figure out as we can and order as we will with the help of our shepherds and with the tools provided by such things as law, science, philosophy, and the sense God gave a goose—all with the help of the Spirit, of course.

That means we may have strong views on Harry Potter, smoking, health care, the Iraq war, weight loss, and even how those with same-sex attraction may order their lives in society (short of perverting the sacrament of marriage). But the Church is not going to micromanage our views on those things—and it never has. That's why you had great saints on both sides of the Avignon schism, the Civil War, the Galileo controversy, the question of the merits of St. Thomas Aquinas's work, and every other serious controversy that has faced the world since the birth of the Church. And it's why you have Catholics arguing about homeschooling, whether BP or big government is the villain in the Great Spill of 2010, whether we should institute carbon credits, and whether government health-care legislation is a good idea.

In short, rarely will the Church hand down dogma. Virtually always, when it comes to moral acts, she hands down a few elementary moral truths such as "don't murder" and "love your enemy," and then she hands down finely crafted *counsel* steeped in the tradition of the Church so that we might apply such teaching to our circumstances. She simply does not live (and never has) by the motto "That which is not forbidden is compulsory."

That's the basic difference between ideology and the Catholic faith. The faith says, "We don't know much, but we do know that *these* few things that God has revealed are true." Ideology, in contrast, claims to be an all-explaining theory of everything. Ideology (which is to say, "heresy") seeks to whittle ultimate reality (that is, God) down to size and make him manageable—in a word, an idol. That's why it's crucial to remember that God is more *unlike* than *like* any creature. St. Thomas Aquinas tells us:

> Although it may be admitted that creatures are in some sort like God, it must nowise be admitted that God is like creatures; because, as Dionysius says (*Div. Nom.* ix): "A mutual likeness may be found between things of the same order, but not between a cause and that which is caused." For, we say that a statue is like a man, but not conversely; so also a creature can be spoken of as in some sort like God; but not that God is like a creature.[5]

The Catholic faith says that things are like God but denies that God is like things. Faith lets God be God and reveal himself on *his* terms—which are, paradoxically, *our* terms in the Incarnation of God as man in Christ Jesus.

Because of this, the Church has never had a problem with doubt, provided it is *honest* doubt. Indeed, the Church has deep compassion for doubters, since the gospel, after all, was forged in a crucible of doubt. John the Baptist doubted both Jesus and himself, asking, "Are you he who is to come, or shall we look for another?" (Matthew 11:3). Note that Jesus did not rebuke the honest doubts clouding John's thoughts as, awaiting execution, John sat in prison. As God bucked up an exhausted and despondent Elijah with his still small voice, so Jesus fed John's flagging faith by reminding him of the solid facts:

> Go and tell John what you hear and see: the blind receive
> their sight and the lame walk, lepers are cleansed and the
> deaf hear, and the dead are raised up, and the poor have good
> news preached to them. And blessed is he who takes no
> offense at me. (Matthew 11:4–6)

More than this, he took the occasion not to diss John the Baptist as
a weakling lacking true faith but to praise him to the crowds:

> As they went away, Jesus began to speak to the crowds con-
> cerning John: "What did you go out into the wilderness to
> behold? A reed shaken by the wind? Why then did you go
> out? To see a man dressed in soft robes? Behold, those who
> wear soft robes are in kings' houses. Why then did you go
> out? To see a prophet? Yes, I tell you, and more than a
> prophet. This is he of whom it is written,
>
> 'Behold, I send my messenger before your face, who shall
> prepare your way before you.'
>
> Truly, I say to you, among those born of women there has
> arisen no one greater than John the Baptist." (Matthew
> 11:7–11)

Nor was John the last doubter. As Jesus himself warned his disciples, including the famous doubting Thomas, on Holy Thursday,
"You will all fall away" (Matthew 26:31). And that warning of terrifying thunderbolts and long rainy days of doubt has been the
Christian experience ever since. Whether in the process of conversion, when we discover with Paul how hard it is "to kick against the
goads" (Acts 26:14), or at some point in our Christian life, the overwhelming majority of us experience doubt sooner or later, and

usually several times. It may be doubt about God's existence or goodness. It may be doubt about Jesus Christ. It may be doubt about the Church, or the Bible, or some aspect of their teaching. It may be doubt about yourself or something that has constituted a sure anchor for your soul. It may steal over the soul with the accumulation of thoughts and feelings you don't know what to do with. It may be pounded into your heart with a nail by the shock of tragedy or betrayal. But however it comes, it must be faced with the help of Jesus Christ through his body the Church.

Doubts can be located in the emotions, intellect, or will. Emotional doubts can be potent, but very often, when you interrogate them, there's no "there" there at all. Those who seek to counsel the doubtful can often be of tremendous help simply by listening and letting the doubtful one speak his feelings aloud so that simple sunlight dissipates the emotional doubt. The doubt he had about the new job turns out to be rooted not in reality but in the fact that it plucked the string of some half-forgotten childhood trauma. Once that comes out into the light, he can move on.

Sometimes doubts arise from real and reasonable questions. If the Church is guided by the Spirit, why did the priest scandal happen? If the Bible is inerrant, how come it says the world was made in six days? If God called me to marry this woman, how come I'm so attracted to that one? None of these are forbidden questions. All of them need to be addressed in some way. And indeed, the classic manner in which Christian philosophy came to treat of everything from soup to nuts is a great deal more thorough than we generally like.

St. Thomas Aquinas, for instance, carefully and methodically addressed thousands upon thousands of doubts about the faith fearlessly and with the enthusiastic approval of the allegedly obscurantist Church that was allegedly terrified of the human mind. He knew—as the apostles knew—that the faith had walked out of the grave and therefore had nothing to fear from the truth. Indeed, even by St. Thomas's day, that faith was already an anvil that had worn out a thousand hammers. So he interrogated it for all it was worth.

In contrast, turn on the TV that so often boasts we live in an age of reason that has triumphed over the dark ages of faith. You will find that what in our civilization passes for "asking tough questions" consists of people shouting past each other with sound bites and accusations, then breaking for the sacred commercial. A medieval *disputatio* would bore a TV producer to tears. Our media don't want to *argue* (a word derived from the Latin for "to clarify"). They want noise to attract a crowd so that they might accomplish their real purpose: selling beer and shampoo. That's the difference between the Age of Faith and our supposed age of reason: Medievals used the intellect; our age merely worships it.

The Catholic Church still lives in the Age of Faith. Therefore it believes that, with the help of the Spirit, an intellectual fault can be dealt with by learning to think and getting decent information. Those seeking to counsel the doubtful must therefore be willing to roll up their sleeves and do the hard work of thinking as best they can. Pietistic bromides like "It's not ours to question" are not Catholic. On the contrary, it is emphatically ours to question long and hard until we've gotten an answer. "It is," says Proverbs 25:2, "the glory of God to conceal things, / but the glory of kings is to search things out."

We are to worship God with our *minds* as well as our hearts. So the cry that the living God show his face—the intellectual hunger to come to the *resolution* of doubt—is a perfectly legitimate thing. As Chesterton said, "The object of opening the mind, as of opening the mouth, is to shut it again on something solid."[6] Those who counsel the doubtful should not squelch that doubt with false piety but help direct the doubtful to the only thing that can satisfy them: truth. The truth may well turn out to be (and in the case of God *will* turn out to be) a mystery so bright that it cannot be comprehended fully by the intellect. But the problem will be too much light, not too little. The healthy intellect can accept such an arrangement and say, "It is enough, Lord."

That said, there is a place where doubt *can* cut itself off from the power of mere counsel to help. This is when doubt is located not in the intellect but in the will. He who says, "I believe that I may understand," is living a healthy intellectual life. He is asking questions to find things out. But when a person begins asking questions to *keep* from finding things out, no counsel will help. All that is left is prayer for a miraculous act of conversion (or reconversion) by the Holy Spirit. That's what Paul warns about when he speaks of those who are "ever learning and never able to come to the knowledge of the truth" (2 Timothy 3:7, *KJV*).

It's a technique we seem tempted by from infancy. Here's a kid staving off bedtime by asking endless questions while ignoring the answers. He's not interested in truth. He's interested in keeping

Mom from turning out the lights. A few years later he deploys his best tree-house lawyer skills to argue that, although Dad told him to stop bothering his sister, he requires definition about precisely *which* side of the car is his. It's all so confusing! Does poking her leg meet the technical definition of "bothering," or is it merely a friendly gesture she is choosing to misinterpret? Not long after, he is in a sophomore moral-theology class, suggesting ingenious posers like "If I could save someone's life by cheating on a test in this class, then couldn't we say that cheating in this class is a *good* thing?"

A few years later, that boy is a young married man asking himself, "How far can I go with my secretary before it's technically, precisely, 'adultery' or 'fornication'? This is so confusing! I doubt there's an answer to this mystery! I guess I'll just have to be loving toward her on those late nights at the office." When his wife finally confronts him after the secretary turns up at the door pregnant, we find our hero saying, "I believe in the primacy of *conscience*, not in some fading rules in a catechism. I don't think I owe anyone an apology."

Note the technique deployed first in the service of venial and finally of mortal sin: Ask questions, not to find anything out but to *keep* from finding anything out. The problem is not honest doubt centered in an intellect seeking light, but dishonest doubt centered in a will seeking darkness. It is ordered toward deliberately making nonsense, rather than sense, out of obvious moral teaching.

The Church rejects such games. She gives us a relatively small number of rock-bottom truths about God, the human person, how we should worship, how we should act, and how we should pray. Things like "You shall not commit adultery" and "Avoid near occasions of sin." Beyond that, she asks us to form our hearts, minds, and bodies in light of those rock-bottom truths, while acknowledging that things can get enormously complex, sticky, ambiguous, and conflicted. In short, the Church is the original practitioner of a theology of doubt. Only the thing she urges us to doubt is not the small body of dogma entrusted to her care but our own ability to squeeze God into our heads or whittle him down to fit our political, cultural, sexual, social, philosophical, and financial demands.

That's because the problem of doubt centered in the will is not lack of information but mule-headed refusal to embrace the bleedin' obvious. When such a perverted will becomes acute, it can destroy a soul completely, as Jesus warned the Pharisees whose wills so twisted their intellects that they declared, "It is only by Be-el'zebul, the prince of demons, that this man casts out demons" (Matthew 12:24). As C.S. Lewis sagely observed of Uncle Andrew, "The trouble about trying to make yourself stupider than you really are is that you very often succeed."[7]

Such persistence in seeking darkness is the radical sickness of soul that prompts Jesus to say, "Do not give dogs what is holy; and do not throw your pearls before swine, lest they trample them under foot and turn to attack you" (Matthew 7:6). When it is a perverted will that "questions" in order to refuse light rather than seek it, wisdom says to the one who counsels the doubtful, "Don't beat your head against the wall. This kind does not come out except by prayer and fasting."

Thanks be to God, though, many doubters are more like Thomas than like the hardened Pharisees. How do we begin to help these honest doubters? Speaking of Lewis, his other famous uncle (Screwtape) gives us the best backhanded advice here. Our infernal correspondent says:

> The Enemy loves platitudes. Of a proposed course of action He wants men, so far as I can see, to ask very simple questions; is it righteous? is it prudent? is it possible? Now if we can keep men asking "Is it in accordance with the general movement of our time? Is it progressive or reactionary? Is this the way that History is going?" they will neglect the relevant questions. And the questions they *do* ask are, of course, unanswerable; for they do not know the future, and what the future will be depends very largely on just those choices which they now invoke the future to help them to make. As a result, while their minds are buzzing in this vacuum, we have the better chance to slip in and bend them to the action we have decided on.[8]

When in doubt, start with the platitudes, the same old stuff, the ordinary teaching of the Church, the common sense, the stuff your mother taught you, the next practical thing, and the cry "Help me, God!" Above all, draw near to God, his body the Church, and the sacraments, not away from them. Just as your body needs sufficient food, rest, play, and work, so your spirit does too. Feed on the Eucharist; rest in the revelation of Christ; get counsel from a priest, spiritual director, or wise person. Play with the questions you have by bouncing them off others who have the information and the wisdom to help you find your answers. And give your spirit a workout by not getting distracted from your day-to-day duties of obedience to Christ and winding up with your mind "buzzing in a vacuum." If you are counseling others, don't try to be a hero if you genuinely can't help. The great thing about being Catholic is that you don't have to know it all. It's a big Church with a lot of resources to draw on. Odds are good that any doubt a person struggles with has already been chewed over in minute detail by somebody else somewhere in the Church's theological and pastoral treasury of experience. Learn how to find information (starting with the *Catechism*).

The great blessing of God's strange gift of doubt is that, as with the stranger gift of exercise, you slowly build up "muscles" over time. You discover that the house built on the rock is not shaken by the storm of doubt. You realize your faith did not shatter. You see once more that the Church's teaching and the wisdom of God are sensible and beautiful. And you find that Blessed John Henry Newman was simply being accurate when he famously observed, "Ten thousand difficulties do not make one doubt."[9]

Admonish the Sinner

O<small>F ALL THE WORKS OF</small> mercy, probably the most thankless and despised is admonishing the sinner. Nobody wants to do it (except human toothaches), and people never want it done to them.

Repent! is a word that eats at the heart. Your conscience nags, "Who are *you*, you great hypocritical gasbag, to go all John-the-Baptist on people?" Here you are, riddled with a thousand sins and vices that leave you in no position to mind anybody else's business. But then something sticks in your craw, and the Holy Spirit won't let you rest.

You can't bear the way that guy humiliates his wife and kids in public. You watch the news and hear some politician lie through his teeth about the graft you know for a fact is happening down at city hall. That woman at work unloads on you with her bigoted remarks about coworkers, behind their backs. Your shoulder angel looks at you with a cocked eyebrow and says, "Well? You gonna let that stand?"

Throughout life we find ourselves facing evil—sometimes obvious, sometimes subtle—and either not quite knowing what to do about it or being afraid to do what we should. That's because another imperative is drilled into us, not just by our Christian background but also by our relativist culture, which regards only one biblical passage as divinely inspired: "Judge not, that you be not judged" (Matthew 7:1).

The problem with invoking this as the Only Thing Jesus Ever Said is that it isn't the only thing he ever said. Still less was it ever intended by him as a commandment to make no moral evaluations or to not speak in the face of obvious evil. The proof of this is Jesus himself, who not only makes moral judgments frequently but urges us to do the same: "Do not judge by appearances, but judge with right judgment" (John 7:24).

The commandment against judging is not an exhortation to never make moral judgments (a feat that is, in any case, impossible). It is an exhortation to remember that, though we are creatures who by nature make moral judgments, we must always recall that such judgments are *provisional*, since we are not God. We can (and should) say that a woman who beats her child black and blue is doing evil. But we cannot say for certain what lies in the heart of such a woman, what terrible demons, sickness, or suffering may be the genesis of her crime, or what her interior freedom was as she acted, or what her eternal destiny may be. Instead of setting ourselves up as her superiors and gloating over her fate, we had best be praying for her, warning her away from such evil, taking the appropriate steps to stop her (including calling the cops), and hoping that she will come to know the healing love of God.

Admonishing the sinner, then, is not an act of cold pharisaic pride but an act of genuine Christian love. It is always ordered toward hoping for the best, even when there is, to the mortal eye, nothing left to hope for. And that is often the case with the prophets. Here, for example, is the rather deflating mission statement God gives to Isaiah at the start of his ministry:

> And I heard the voice of the Lord saying, "Whom shall I send, and who will go for us?" Then I said, "Here am I! Send me." And he said,
>
> "Go, and say to this people: / 'Hear and hear, but do not understand; / see and see, but do not perceive.' / Make the heart of this people fat, / and their ears heavy, / and shut their eyes; / lest they see with their eyes, / and hear with their ears, / and understand with their hearts, / and turn and be healed." / Then I said, "How long, O Lord?" / And he said: "Until cities lie waste / without inhabitant, / and houses without men, / and the land is utterly desolate, / and the LORD removes men far away, / and the forsaken places are many in the midst of the land. / And though a tenth remain in it, / it will be burned again, / like a terebinth or an oak, / whose stump remains standing / when it is felled." / The holy seed is its stump. (Isaiah 6:8–13)

"You will do your best and you will fail!" is not the message we want to hear. But it's the bitterly realistic message Isaiah received at the inauguration of his work. Being told that the overwhelming majority of your audience is going to ignore you and perish, that the ones who don't perish will also ignore you and then "be burned again," and that, finally, some tiny stump will be left—well, that's not the successful vision statement we normally expect from the divine recruitment brochure.

It is, however, what the prophets of Israel and what the Christian martyrs, following their Lord, signed on for. And the retirement plan?

> Some were tortured, refusing to accept release, that they might rise again to a better life. Others suffered mocking and scourging, and even chains and imprisonment. They were stoned, they were sawn in two, they were killed with the sword; they went about in skins of sheep and goats, destitute, afflicted, ill-treated—of whom the world was not worthy—wandering over deserts and mountains, and in dens and caves of the earth. (Hebrews 11:35–38)

Good times, good times. As the prophets and martyrs testified, by their blood, admonishing the sinner is a fine way to get rejected and tortured to death by the admonished. For it is the nature of pride—that is, the root of all sin—that the more deeply enmeshed you are in it, the less you want to hear from people who are calling you to repent of it.

Conversely, it is the nature of the prophetic office that the worse the sin is, the more the prophet feels a burden to speak out against it. That burden may lead to a more terrible conflict than the one between the admonisher and the admonished. It can lead to the torments Jeremiah described as he struggled under (1) the burden God laid on him, (2) his own frustration at his failures, (3) the hostility of sinners, and (4) his own deepest awareness that God is trustworthy, despite all the torments he might be enduring:

O LORD, you have deceived me, / and I was deceived; / you are stronger than I, / and you have prevailed. / I have become a laughingstock all the day; / every one mocks me. / For whenever I speak, I cry out, / I shout, "Violence and destruction!" / For the word of the LORD has become for me / a reproach and derision all day long. / If I say, "I will not mention him, / or speak any more in his name," / there is in my heart as it were a burning fire / shut up in my bones, / and I am weary with holding it in, / and I cannot. / For I hear many whispering. / Terror is on every side! / "Denounce him! Let us denounce him!" / say all my familiar friends, / watching for my fall. / "Perhaps he will be deceived, / then we can overcome him, / and take our revenge on him." / But the LORD is with me as a dread warrior; / therefore my persecutors will stumble, / they will not overcome me. / They will be greatly shamed, / for they will not succeed. / Their eternal dishonor / will never be forgotten. / O LORD of hosts, who test the righteous, / who sees the heart and the mind, / let me see your vengeance upon them, / for to you have I committed my cause. / Sing to the LORD; / praise the LORD! / For he has delivered the life of the needy / from the hand of evildoers. / Cursed be the day / on which I was born! / The day when my mother bore me, / let it not be blessed! / Cursed be the man / who brought the news to my father, / "A son is born to you," / making him very glad. / Let that man be like the cities / which the LORD overthrew without pity; / let him hear a cry in the morning / and an alarm at noon, / because he did not kill me in the womb; / so my mother would have been my grave, / and her womb for ever great. / Why did I come forth from the womb / to see toil and sorrow, / and spend my days in shame? (Jeremiah 20:7–18)

And so, down through the ages, people arise, filled with a burning-in-the-bone sense that they must speak out and admonish the sinner, for God himself requires it. Indeed, he requires it so seriously that if the prophet does not speak, he knows he himself will be held responsible for the sinner should he not discharge his duty:

Son of man, I have made you a watchman for the house of Israel; whenever you hear a word from my mouth, you shall give them warning from me. If I say to the wicked, "You shall surely die," and you give him no warning, nor speak to warn the wicked from his wicked way, in order to save his life, that wicked man shall die in his iniquity; but his blood I will require at your hand. But if you warn the wicked, and he does not turn from his wickedness, or from his wicked way, he shall die in his iniquity; but you will have saved your life. Again, if a righteous man turns from his righteousness and commits iniquity, and I lay a stumbling block before him, he shall die; because you have not warned him, he shall die for his sin, and his righteous deeds which he has done shall not be remembered; but his blood I will require at your hand. Nevertheless if you warn the righteous man not to sin, and he does not sin, he shall surely live, because he took warning; and you will have saved your life. (Ezekiel 3:17–21)

Of course, along with true prophets there are always pretenders shouting about some evil or other, not for the sake of the kingdom of God, nor even for the good of their neighbor, but because they are busybodies, social climbers, political adventurers, or the next tyrant. Sometimes it's pretty easy to spot the phony. The politician profiled in "Won't Get Fooled Again," by the Who, denouncing his opponent only to continue his corrupt policies, is not admonishing sinners but merely playing for power. Likewise, a pundit who gins up panic about the economy and then admonishes his viewers to invest in the gold company for which he is spokesman is a huckster, not a prophet. Similarly, the celebrity who takes private jets around the world to denounce global warming is merely being fashionable.

The busybody, likewise, cares little for the repentance of the sinner, since his true delight is in the impenitence of the sinner. After all, if the sinner repents, what will there be to gossip about? One particularly noxious species of busybody is the Christian who urges us to "pray" for so-and-so—and then proceeds, not to pray, but to rehearse the sins of the sinner with barely concealed delectation.

Another example of false admonishment (though with a somewhat more redeeming quality) is the guy who plays at being bravely "prophetic" as he stays safely cocooned in his little peer group, issuing thundering denunciations of Them (whoever They are). To be sure, there's sometimes a place for bucking up the home team with reminders about the sins of Those Bad People Over There and the fact that we good guys need to fight them. Allied propaganda that reminded our citizenry that the Axis powers were evil and needed to be defeated was not wrong. But it was not "brave" for a man in an office in Washington, D.C., to write that propaganda, and his writing was not admonishment of the sinner but rather performance art in the service of unit cohesion.

The reason it is important to distinguish team-building propaganda from admonishment is simply this: One is often tempted to excuse one's own evil by comparing oneself with Those Bad People Over There. Not everybody who bucks up the home team is acting from noble motives. The proof of this is that the Axis powers had *their* propaganda too and tried to justify their evils by pointing to our faults as well. They were not admonishing anybody. They were justifying their own crimes by poisoning their citizens' minds against people they had never met, would never communicate with, and about whom they knew nothing but what the state fed them.

On a much smaller scale, we can do the same thing: We can gossip about "those people" and tell our inner circle what jerks they are— pretending we are bravely admonishing the sinner when all we are doing is indulging in a mutual-admiration society with our friends at the expense of those we dislike.

The point is this: Admonishing the sinner means *confronting* the sinner, not gossiping about him behind his back. Moreover, for the Catholic, it means confronting him in light of Christ's revelation, rooted in that hope that he is capable of moral reasoning and repentance by the power of the Spirit.

We are well on the way to abandoning that hope. Our manufacturers of culture—left and right—speak as though an opponent can be motivated only by a sort of subhuman stupidity or malice impervious to moral reasoning. Liberals and conservatives in pop media routinely fulfill Godwin's law, a puckish "rule" of Internet discourse: "As an online discussion grows longer, the probability of a comparison involving Nazis or Hitler approaches." Everybody from Bush to Obama to NPR to Fox News winds up being Hitler for fifteen minutes.

This lazy tendency to indulge in tribal vilification instead of admonishment is, of course, nothing new. In the New Testament, Jesus had to oppose such attitudes not only in his enemies but in his friends. He broke social and cultural barriers constantly and amazed or appalled both the Pharisees and the apostles. He ate with tax collectors and prostitutes, talked to Roman soldiers, consorted with lepers, took former terrorists like Simon the Zealot as his disciples, and befriended dodgy women with unpromising psychological profiles, such as Mary Magdalene, "from whom he had cast out seven demons" (Mark 16:9). It's therefore not surprising that the Pharisees' spiritual laziness—which caused them to strain at gnats such as hand washings and to swallow camels such as hypocrisy, malice, and pride—also caused them to act supremely lazy by harshly judging him. He ate with tax collectors and sinners. 'Nuff said. There was nobody there for the Pharisees to know: just an enemy to be ignored and—when he criticized them—to kill.

Lest we moderns gloat over the foolish Pharisees too much, however, we should note that postmodernity has contributed something new but not improved to this ancient evil of spiritual laziness. Postmoderns have added to the ancient tribalism of the Pharisee another very significant reason for the abandonment of admonishment: our rejection of the reality of sin.

Rejecting the reality of sin, we have ended up abandoning the hope of repentance. When you reject the idea of common truth, prattling that "truth is whatever is true for you," you reject the basis for reason and argument. But you don't (and can't) reject the reality of your anger over sin. You can't ignore it when somebody steals your wallet or beats up your child. But you can pretend that the sinner was an irrational animal acting solely under the influence of genes or environment and not to sin of which he can repent. So we increasingly treat sinners as we treat animals: diagnosing, caging, or killing them like rabid dogs, but never talking about sin or repentance.

The old idea of the penitentiary is almost entirely gone. It is no longer, as the name suggests, a place for penance. It is a state-run warehouse (and slaughterhouse) for human animals who have, as the saying goes, "forfeited their humanity."

It is, of course, possible to laugh off the notion of repentance as hopelessly Pollyanna and caricature it as the naēve belief that hardened thugs will melt into saints if you talk nicely to them. But that's not my point or my claim. It is, rather, that in abandoning our understanding of the human person to the secular state instead of having the courage of our convictions as Catholics, we are laying the foundation for treating *all* human beings as animals and potential criminals rather than as citizens of a free society. One need only note the changes in our security state over the past ten years. Big Brother has eyes everywhere. In airports and public facilities across America, Boy Scouts, nuns, and little old ladies from Lake Wobegon are expected to endure invasive searches that, in any other context, should result in an arrest for sexual predation. An eighty-six-year-old bedridden woman is Tasered (twice) while the cops stand on her oxygen hose and her protesting grandson is cuffed and frog-marched out of the house. The cops explain that it was all justified because she "took a more aggressive posture in her bed." The idea that she was a human being never entered their heads. [1]

The curious result of our culture's growing abandonment of the notion of sin is (as Faustian bargains tend to be) a loss of our humanity. As we become coarser and our belief that humans are made in the image of God fades to a theory of humans as animals shaped by heredity and environment, our faith in the power of moral suasion goes with it. So, for instance, a majority of Americans (including, alas, Catholics) forget our successful use of conventional interrogation with Nazis and Communists and embrace the lie that intelligence can best be gained from enemy combatants via "enhanced interrogation" (a euphemism for torture). This is a complete rejection of the Church's teaching on human dignity and is founded on the assertion that human beings are, at bottom, beasts.[2] Eventually it occurs to Caesar that if "enhanced interrogation" may be used on perceived *foreign* threats, then why not on *domestic* ones too? Enhanced interrogation begins to be deployed to interrogate not merely suspected terrorists abroad but also suspected criminals at home.

In short, as a culture embraces the view that men are brutes, it is not possible to keep that genie in the bottle of a CIA black site. Caesar inevitably starts to treat his subjects that way too. He abandons the language of a ruler maintaining ordered liberty for a free people and speaks more and more like a bureaucrat barking threats at contemptible servants—or cracking whips at beasts. So, for instance, where there used to be public-service announcements saying, "Every litter bit hurts," we now get "Litter and it will hurt." "Buckle up for safety!" has been replaced with "Click it or ticket!" "Friends don't let friends drive drunk" is replaced by "Drive hammered. Get nailed." Threats, not admonishment, are the order of the day.

The apotheosis of such contempt-based social control in media (so far) is the infamous "No Pressure" ad sponsored by 10:10, an organized campaign to reduce carbon emissions. There was no attempt to admonish by saying, "Even if you are skeptical about anthropogenic global warming, it couldn't hurt if we all pitched in and cared for the environment as best we can." That would respect human dignity. Instead the ad (which its makers actually imagined was funny) shows an elementary-school teacher urging her class to reduce their carbon footprint. When two children express reservations, the teacher mildly says, "No pressure," and then pushes a large red button on her desk, whereupon the nonconforming kids explode in bloody chunks, splattering the other screaming children in the classroom. This revolting gag is repeated a few more times to drive home the message: Submit to the Religion of Anthropogenic Climate Change or be slaughtered like animals.[3]

If Christ is to be believed, all this violent contempt for human dignity is foreign to what we actually are. Why do we prefer to treat people like animals when, in fact, admonishing the sinner and not stampeding the herd is truer to our nature as rational beings?

Answer: because admonishing the sinner is hard. Christ did it, and it got him nailed to a cross. For admonishment means looking somebody in the eye rather than imposing bureaucratic solutions from three thousand miles away. It means addressing a fellow human being as an equal, not a lab rat, sheep, or contagion. It means stating truly unpopular opinions, not to peers who share them but to enemies who don't. It means the risk of losing friends, family, job, and reputation. It means speaking about things that are awkward and uncomfortable. And in our post-Christian world, it often means doing it in a grammar and terminology that members of our culture know, if at all, only in a sort of pidgin.

I know only a few replies to the person who says, "Then I think I'd rather not." One is this: You should anyway, if for no other reason than that you will sleep better at night. Another is this: Sometimes when you admonish the sinner, he repents—because the sinner still has a conscience, heart, and soul. Some of the moments I am most thankful for are those when a friend who truly loved me took me aside and, with tears glistening in her eyes, said, "Mark, I wouldn't want to hurt you for the world. But when you did X, you really disappointed me. I know you are better than that! Repent, ask forgiveness, and right the wrong you did." Half the time my conscience was nagging me before my friend spoke. It was a relief to admit the sin.

In such cases admonishment is particularly revealed for what it is: not a shattering blow designed to humiliate and destroy the sinner but a reassuring reminder that, heinous as we both know this sin was, God is not abandoning the sinner but is calling him back to mercy and restoration. Indeed, many, many times admonishing the sinner means admonishing him not to despair over his sin.

The hope of our tradition is very simple: It is that God saves sinners—real, nasty, repulsive sinners—and not merely colorfully charming golden-hearted rogues from comic burlesques who drink a bit, like the sight of a pretty pair of legs, and wouldn't harm a flea. It is a faith rooted in the R-rated spectacle of the life of King David, a power-drunk despot who used his clout to steal a good man's wife, impregnate her, and then murder the victim of his despicable crime by trading on his very loyalty to send him into battle for his king— and abandon him there. In any other oriental despotism of antiquity, confronting the man who committed such a crime would have meant instant death. But when the prophet Nathan admonished David, something extraordinary occurred. David sagged on his throne and, instead of having Nathan executed as an example to his court, sobbed, "I have sinned against the LORD" (2 Samuel 12:13). Then he composed one of the greatest poems of antiquity. It's a beacon of hope to every sinner who has ever lived after him. It reads in part:

> Have mercy on me, O God, according to your merciful love;
>   according to your abundant mercy blot out my
>   transgressions.
> Wash me thoroughly from my iniquity,
> and cleanse me from my sin!
> …
> Create in me a clean heart, O God,
>   and put a new and right spirit within me.
> Cast me not away from your presence,
>   and take not your holy Spirit from me.

> Restore to me the joy of your salvation,
>
> and uphold me with a willing spirit. (Psalm 51:1–2, 10–12)

That psalm stands as a permanent reminder of the power of the Holy Spirit, even at this hour, to change the world when a disciple of Jesus calls a sinner to doff the mask of sin and become who he really is: a child of God in the image of Christ.

CHAPTER 11

Bear Wrongs Patiently

*F*OR ME TO ASSUME THE task of writing about "bearing wrongs patiently" is like asking the Incredible Hulk for anger-management counseling. I don't bear wrongs patiently. Why should I? Those people are *wrong*! They need to be set right! I'm only doing my Christian duty of admonishing the sinner when I inform that jerk that he's a jerk. I'm not indulging the sin of anger! I'm Jesus in the temple, taking a rope of cords to the money changers! Anybody who gets in my way is certainly not asking me to bear wrongs patiently or lovingly rebuking my unjust anger. He is a wishy-washy *coward* cringing in the face of real evil and is going all Neville Chamberlain when what is needed is righteous wrath!

You laugh. But that's how it feels when you are in the grip of vengefulness, and it's why "bearing wrongs patiently" is so hard. And don't kid me. You're no different—and with good reason.

The reason you are no different is that this work of mercy is not called "bear *imagined* wrongs patiently." It's talking about *real wrongs*, when the other guy really *is* a dirtbag who, very deliberately and with sociopathic malice aforethought, publicly slanders, yells at, and reduces to tears a good Christian widow with small children, all because of his envy of her and his own rankling (and richly deserved) sense of inferiority. It's talking about when some bitter little twerp publicly attacks a holy old priest and lies about him with granite impenitence. It's talking about that punk kid who keyed your car and got away before you could get his license. It's talking about the cancer your kid sister got, despite years of healthy living. It's talking about that person (*you* know who) who did that awful thing that one time and who not only has never apologized but still likes to remind you of how he embarrassed and hurt you. It's talking about everything that has ever happened to you or those you love that was truly unjust, unfair, and *wrong*.

Now, I know, as you probably do, those people who really seem to be able to bear such things patiently—saints, both living and dead, who have encountered great tragedies or, what is sometimes harder to bear, small and persistent misfortunes and annoyances, and yet come out the other side praising God and full of joy.

I'm not one of them (though I hope in God that this will eventually change). I can hardly deal with mere misfortunes, much less sins against me. Indeed, I find misfortune in some ways more difficult. After all, when humans hurt me it can at least be chalked up to free will and sins against a good God who didn't want to see me harmed. But when life just sets me up for some random accidental misfortune, my mind almost instantly goes into full Job mode. My immediate temptation is to listen to the hissing voice that says, "God is not here, and besides, he is evil. He's laughing at your cosmic pie in the face! He does this for his sport!"

When the wrong that I must bear patiently happens because God, in his providence, let it happen, it *feels* like God is playing a cruel joke. So I become a seething cauldron of anger at God, and counsels to "bear it patiently" strike my sinful ears like the sick counsels of an abusive parent saying, "Smile! Daddy beats you because you cry so much."

Not that my response to human sin is much better. Generally, my reaction to those who sin against me and those I love is to grind my teeth and take walks or showers, during which I formulate the perfect riposte. Recently I was fantasizing about throwing a drink in somebody's face if I ever had the misfortune to meet him in person. On my weaker days I let fly with words calculated to hurt. On my stronger days I simply stew in my juices and have to work long and hard to really hand those people over to God and ask that they be forgiven. And even then I have my strategies for clinging to anger.

I'm enough of a Christian to know the extremely unpleasant teaching of our Lord:

> For if you forgive men their trespasses, your heavenly Father also will forgive you; but if you do not forgive men their trespasses, neither will your Father forgive your trespasses. (Matthew 6:14–15)

I'm also a clever enough Christian that I can often fool myself (though not God, I am sorry to say) into believing that so long as I cherish hatred against a person when he or she wrongs *somebody else*, then I am being a noble knight defending the honor of a friend and am not looking for an excuse for the sin of anger and a chance to kick butt. Like many others, I am tempted to pretend that I am under no obligation to forgive people who sin against those I care about. I like to forget, as most people like to forget, that if the guy who robbed my friend is on the receiving end of my anger for his act of theft against my friend, then I have likewise assumed my friend's obligation to forgive him. As Jesus says:

> And whenever you stand praying, forgive, if you have *anything against any one*; so that your Father also who is in heaven may forgive you your trespasses. (Mark 11:25, emphasis mine)

There are lots of other tricks for avoiding the terrible command to forgive. One is to conflate forgiveness with inaction, as though forgiving somebody means doing nothing about the evil he or she commits. It is a standard straw-man argument that we Vengies like to tell ourselves just before we run off to commit the opposite evil of clinging to bitterness. It goes like this:

We tell ourselves (in the tone of voice we reserve for saying, "You just stirred my tea with your used Q-Tip"), "*Merciful* people—those gooey peace 'n' justice types—are nothing but pacifist bed wetters who allow evil to go unchallenged. They are enablers of evil. Mercy for Osama bin Laden? Forgiveness for some molesting monster like Marcial Maciel Degollado? Outrageous!"

It's an inviting and easy thing to say. Murderers escape justice, and not a few abusive priests have managed to avoid the just punishment of the law because somebody thought it would be "unforgiving" to call the cops. We *know* that this is rubbish and feel the frustration of any morally sane person at passivity in the face of such evil. We know perfectly well that the task of the Christian in such a situation is to report the crime to the police lest other innocents suffer. Forgiveness, we shout in exasperation, does *not* equal passivity.

But then we make the fatal error. We go on to imagine that suckling at the breast of fury and unforgiveness constitutes "doing something" about priest abuse, or terrorism, or whatever other evil.

The reality is that unforgiveness does nothing whatsoever to defeat evil or establish justice. It does not get rid of bad clerics, help victims, stop terrorism, or bring a single person closer to God or to the communion of saints. The only actual, practical results of unforgiveness are that people are filled with bitterness, hold an ever weaker grip on their faith, "encourage" one another to consider the possibility of schism and hatred of their country or the enemy, and nurture an ever deeper cynicism. St. James is right: "The anger of man does not work the righteousness of God" (James 1:20).

Some people play the "I don't have to forgive until my enemy says 'sorry'" game. If we buy that, we must realize we are directly disobeying Jesus Christ, who says, "Love your enemy," not "Love your former enemy." Moreover, we must learn that the punishment for refusing to forgive is the unforgiveness itself. For unforgiveness punishes us, not our enemy. When we refuse to forgive, we hand our happiness over—forever—to people who may not even know we exist, much less care. We chain ourselves to eternal misery and enslave ourselves, often to people long dead. It's folly.

That's why Jesus is right. Refusing to extend forgiveness is one of the most deadly manifestations of pride in the world. It achieves nothing of what it promises ("Someday he'll say he's sorry, and you'll be vindicated for all to see!"), and it ruins not just our lives but the lives of friends and family and all who must suffer our descent into unrequited rage.

Indeed, refusal to forgive trains us for *nothing* but misery. We think we'll find peace when they say they're sorry. But if we've trained ourselves to live in bitterness and cynicism, we'll be stuck there no matter what "they" say (because who can ever believe *them* anyway?). So we hold on to our bitterness. Bottom line: Strength and vindication do not come from refusal to forgive. Nor do safety, security, or any other good things. Only slavery.

The command of Jesus is to *extend* forgiveness to enemies. It is not to pretend the sin never happened. It is not to pretend the impenitent person is penitent. It is not to be nonconfrontational, or sit there and take it, or see no evil. It is not to refuse to take practical action, up to and including jailing or, in a just war, even killing your enemy. But it is to forgive nonetheless. It is to wish their good; to refuse to let cynicism master faith, hope, and charity; to hope for the best while keeping a firm eye on reality. Refusal to extend forgiveness (*extend*, mind you: It is up to the sinner to repent and receive it) does *only* harm—and primarily to the person who refuses to extend forgiveness.

But still we look for strategies to duck forgiveness. We gripe that extending forgiveness means offering "cheap grace." It's the notion that if you don't go on hating that husband who ditched you, if you don't keep repeating to yourself every day the litany of wrongs your mother-in-law has done you, then *your enemy will have gotten away with it!* The crimes will go unpunished if you do not make yourself the Eternal Repository of Memory. The thought "I must not let them off the hook!" sums this up. In reality, what it means is that you are drinking poison and expecting the other person to die.

Some people chew their cud over sickening headlines about sins in some other part of the world and rationalize this as "bearing wrong patiently." If they were doing penance, that could be helpful. But the sort of person I mean often completely neglects prayer and fasting. Instead they simply load themselves with rage and worry about evils that do not involve them and that they cannot possibly affect (except with their neglected prayers for justice and mercy). They dwell in a fantasy world where they imagine that cursing at a computer screen or TV will somehow cure the world's ills. But somebody swearing at her TV in Ohio over some sin committed in Boston or Iran does absolutely nothing except corrode her own soul.

In short, our forgiveness must be modeled on God, who "shows his love for us in that while we were yet sinners Christ died for us" (Romans 5:8) and commands us to do the same. That is what "Love your enemies" means. It doesn't mean "Love people who pay back your emotional bank account by saying they are sorry, thus assuaging your rage." It means "Extend unconditional love and forgiveness to nasty people who despise you and want to harm you. Desire their happiness. Do not cultivate bitterness against them. Fight their evil actions, when necessary and possible, but do not wish them ill."

That's why bearing wrongs patiently is hard. The command to bear wrongs patiently is, quite simply, the command to die, to kill your old self and live to God. It's contrary to every impulse of our fallen human nature, and it both frightens and angers us. It's like being a sheep before his shearers or a lamb led to the slaughter, opening not your mouth. It's like being asked to watch your dearly beloved son go through a kangaroo court and be condemned by jaded and cynical bureaucrats who think nothing of putting him to death in the most horrible and humiliating way possible if only they can cling to their power. It's like being asked to imitate Mary the Mother of Sorrows and her Son, Jesus, who bore our wrongs patiently all the way to his death, even death on a cross.

It is there, on Golgotha alone, that we find the grace from God necessary to bear wrongs patiently. Only there do we discover with clarity that God is not laughing at his dearly beloved Son's misfortunes, or at ours. Only there do the sins of scheming men meet their decisive defeat. Only there do the powers of hell find all evils inverted and turned to God's glory. Only there do we find God himself enduring all the suffering, abandonment, and misfortunes of Job as well as all the spite of men and devils—including our own rage at him for all the evils of the world. And only there can we see the real source of power for all those saints and martyrs who have borne wrongs patiently and, with and in Christ, have seen the fruit of the travail of his soul and been satisfied.

Bearing wrongs patiently is a work of mercy that is possible, in a word, only with the help of Christ crucified. Nobody has ever done it without the grace supplied by his Holy Spirit. That includes non-Christians, because the Light who lightens every person doesn't care about receiving the credit. Many human beings who have been ignorant or even hostile to what they considered his gospel have borne wrongs patiently with the secret help of his Spirit extended to all men of goodwill. For those of us who do know Christ, we have a precious reservoir of grace and power we can draw on—and the knowledge of how badly we need it.

So how do we access that grace? The old advice is best, in my limited experience: Pray as if everything depends on God and act as if
everything depends on you. Or as Paul puts it, "Work out your own
salvation with fear and trembling; for God is at work in you, both to
will and to work for his good pleasure" (Philippians 2:12–13). If you
have trouble bearing wrongs patiently, then do what you can to draw
on the grace of God where it can be found, especially in the sacraments. In particular, Catholics should ask for the gifts of confirma-
tion (which is all about giving disciples of Jesus the power to get up
and do what needs to be done). We should also take our angry resist-
ance to grace and bring it to the sacrament of reconciliation. And of
course, we should go to the Eucharist, pray for those who wrong us,
and ask that the grace of the Eucharist be poured out on them and
those we love.

Another invaluable gift the gospel gives us is a sense of perspective.
Our species has a genius for turning trivialities into world-historical
struggles we kill and die for—and we Christians are not exempt. A
friend who used to amuse himself by reading sundry Christian websites devoted to vicious quarrels over minutiae never forgot the time
some reader asked a site owner if the book of Daniel might date from
the second century BC. The site owner shot back, "THAT IS A LIE FROM
THE PIT OF *HELL*!!!" To those of us outside the bubble of obsession, the
date of the book of Daniel doesn't seem that crucial. But to the
enthusiast it was something worth sacrificing all his love, joy, and
peace on the altar of volcanic rage.

That doesn't happen just on the Internet, of course. Anybody who
has lived in community—whether at home, or in religious life, or in
some sort of private organization—can appreciate the witticism of

Henry Kissinger, that the reason academic quarrels are so bitter is that the stakes are so low.

Jesus himself ups the ante enormously in his demand that we bear wrongs patiently—and then reminds us that the ante is peanuts compared to the wrongs he himself bears. When Peter takes his idea of mercy to the utmost limit and proposes forgiving sins a whopping seven times, Jesus' reply is famous:

> Jesus said to him, "I do not say to you seven times, but seventy times seven.
>
> "Therefore the kingdom of heaven may be compared to a king who wished to settle accounts with his servants. When he began the reckoning, one was brought to him who owed him ten thousand talents; and as he could not pay, his lord ordered him to be sold, with his wife and children and all that he had, and payment to be made. So the servant fell on his knees, imploring him, 'Lord, have patience with me, and I will pay you everything.' And out of pity for him the lord of that servant released him and forgave him the debt. But that same servant, as he went out, came upon one of his fellow servants who owed him a hundred denarii; and seizing him by the throat he said, 'Pay what you owe.' So his fellow servant fell down and besought him, 'Have patience with me, and I will pay you.' He refused and went and put him in prison till he should pay the debt. When his fellow servants saw what had taken place, they were greatly distressed, and they went and reported to their lord all that had taken place. Then his lord summoned him and said to him,

'You wicked servant! I forgave you all that debt because you besought me; and should not you have had mercy on your fellow servant, as I had mercy on you?' And in anger his lord delivered him to the jailers, till he should pay all his debt. So also my heavenly Father will do to every one of you, if you do not forgive your brother from your heart." (Matthew 18:22–35).

This gives us some perspective. When it's *my* soul on the line, I like to remind myself that Jesus bore the sins of Hans Frank, Nazi Gauleiter of Poland, to the cross, so I am pretty small beer in comparison. But when Jesus addresses the question, *I* am the servant who owed the king millions and millions of dollars, while the guy I am ready to choke to death owes me fifty cents.

That's a good place to start: small. Before seeing the guy who took your parking place as the living embodiment of the same kind of evil that overran Europe in 1940, try getting some perspective by saying, "It's just a parking spot. There are plenty more in this town."

St. Thérèse can be very helpful in this regard, because she too had to struggle with bearing extremely small wrongs patiently. Unlike the stonings, horsewhippings, and shipwrecks that characterized the hardships of St. Paul, Thérèse's sufferings ran more toward a sweat of exasperation when the sister next to her rattled her rosary beads during evening prayer. As a general rule, such small stuff is the norm for most of us—and therefore the best place to practice the bearing of wrongs patiently. It's like prepping to run a race. You don't just get up one morning and run a marathon. You start by running short distances and then build up your strength.

Just as the sin of unforgiveness is its own punishment, so the virtue of bearing wrongs patiently is its own reward. It (obviously) doesn't prevent evils from befalling you. But it does transform suffering from meaningless garbage (or worse still, seeming evidence that God has it in for you) into purgatorial pain unto life:

> In your struggle against sin you have not yet resisted to the point of shedding your blood. And have you forgotten the exhortation which addresses you as sons?—"My son, do not regard lightly the discipline of the Lord, nor lose courage when you are punished by him. For the Lord disciplines him whom he loves, and chastises every son whom he receives." It is for discipline that you have to endure. God is treating you as sons; for what son is there whom his father does not discipline? If you are left without discipline, in which all have participated, then you are illegitimate children and not sons. Besides this, we have had earthly fathers to discipline us and we respected them. Shall we not much more be subject to the Father of spirits and live? For they disciplined us for a short time at their pleasure, but he disciplines us for our good, that we may share his holiness. For the moment all discipline seems painful rather than pleasant; later it yields the peaceful fruit of righteousness to those who have been trained by it. Therefore lift your drooping hands and strengthen your weak knees, and make straight paths for your feet, so that what is lame may not be put out of joint but rather be healed. (Hebrews 12:4–13)

In the end, the command to bear wrongs patiently is the command to be like Christ. How telling it is that the sacred writer introduced the subject of suffering by noting that in our struggle with sin we have not yet resisted to the point of shedding blood. That's a deeply Christian observation. Because, in fact, every single disciple of Christ is going to shed his blood for Jesus sooner or later. Not everybody will be physically put to death by sword, bullet, or bomb. Some of us will die in our beds. But all of us will undergo death to self for Christ's sake sooner or later. All of us will take up our cross and follow him—or not. If not, then we will die anyway and experience the second death if we do not repent before our death.

The Greeks said that the love of wisdom is the practice of death. Wisdom enabled Socrates to face his death. It sustained the patriarchs and prophets through their trials. Bearing wrongs patiently is one of the principal pursuits of the wise man, for wisdom means dying and rising with Christ, who is the wisdom and power of God. It was fully displayed in him as he faced the wrongs heaped on him by enemies, friends, and traitors. And it has sustained the martyrs great and small down through time. It is never too soon or too late to try to live it out. Even if you are as miserable at it as I am, we have the great and consoling truth that whatever step we take toward doing it, no matter how feeble, God will honor us with grace to do better next time. For as George MacDonald said, he is easy to please but hard to satisfy.

CHAPTER 12

Forgive Offenses Willingly

THE FORGIVENESS OF SINS, SAID the Fathers of the Church, is a greater miracle than the creation of the universe. That seems exaggerated, when considered from our perspective. A Catholic does something he feels ashamed of, goes in the little room to confession, and comes out a few minutes later. Sometimes he stops for a quick penance prayer in the pew. Sometimes he's off like a shot to his next Saturday afternoon appointment. To the naked eye, it's hard to see this as something akin to God hurling the Andromeda galaxy into being.

And yet, seen from God's perspective, this is what it's all about. The birth at Bethlehem; the life at near-subsistence level; the years of obscurity and hard manual labor; the temptation in the wilderness; the long days and months and years spent wandering and preaching with nowhere to lay his head; the growing hostility, the whispers; the friendship of Judas draining away and leaving only the husk of a smile behind; the incomprehension of the apostles; and, finally, the betrayal, arrest, beatings, crowning with thorns, nakedness, excruciating pain, gasping for breath, isolation, abandonment, and last wrenching moments of agony: It was all to purchase that miracle of forgiveness poured out in that little confessional.

In short, as C.S. Lewis has remarked, it cost God nothing to create nice things. It cost him crucifixion to convert rebellious wills.[1] Those who think of absolution as a sort of magical wave of the hand accomplished with a little ooga booga and sprinkling with magic water simply have no conception of what the mercy really cost.

But why *doesn't* God just do the magic and have done with it? He's God, isn't he? If he can speak being into existence, why *can't* he speak forgiveness into existence without all this blood, smoke, and dust in the drama?

The answer of Catholic tradition is that forgiveness is like epoxy. It has two ingredients, and they must fuse to work. God has to be willing to forgive, but we need to be creatures capable of receiving the forgiveness. Our natures were deformed by the Fall, and the more deformed we are, the less we are capable of receiving what we need: the forgiveness and life of God.

That bit about the "life of God" is important. Because forgiveness is only step one of what God intends to give us. Christ is not merely about bringing our account balance back out of the red and back to zero. Rather, he means to make us into participants in the divine nature (see 2 Peter 1:4). Forgiveness of sins without *divinization* of the human person is just not in the cards in the Christian picture of salvation. We are saved not merely *from* sin but *to* communion with the Blessed Trinity.

That's why God opted not to remain up in heaven and keep things nice and disincarnate. As Athanasius put it, he became man that man might become God.² He assumed our humanity, not merely that he might put the sins of the flesh to death, but so that we might share completely in his divine life. It is this astonishing generosity to our radically unworthy species that the *Exultet* marvels at each Easter: "O happy fault, O necessary sin of Adam, which gained for us so great a Redeemer!"

In the mystery of God's incredible generosity, we find that God actually gives us something better than we would have received had we never sinned. It's as if we robbed a man's house and then found him chasing us down the street, insisting on giving us the jewelry we missed and begging us to marry his daughter. It brings to life in an astonishing way Jesus' strange counsel that if somebody takes your tunic, give him your cloak as well (Matthew 5:40). God gave us his Son, and we killed him. As our reward, he gives us eternal bliss. No wonder Paul said the wisdom of God is foolishness to this world (see 1 Corinthians 1:18–21). It barely escapes being foolishness even to those who believe it.

The command to forgive sins willingly must be seen in light of this incredible and crazy generosity. The operative word here is *willingly*. It's a word with no upper limit. Of course, as we saw in our last chapter, we are in no immediate danger of bumping our heads on any ceiling. Merely acknowledging the command to forgive is often all we can muster. Yet such is the goodness and condescension of God to our weak state that gritting our teeth and saying "I forgive that *jerk*" is gladly reckoned by him as "willing" (much as a parent accepts the efforts of an angry child to be conciliatory even when the kid is still kicking his sister under the table for taking his toy). We have to start somewhere, and God will humble himself to accept our barest attempt at forgiveness, so long as it is a real attempt.

But God is also always saying to us, "You are not nearly as happy as I intend you to be!" Our forgiveness needs to grow, to become more willing, more generous, more joyful at the good of the other. In a word, it must become more godlike, more like him who commends his love to us in that, while we were yet sinners, Christ died for us.

As it happens, we Catholics have been given by God an endless fountain of grace where we get to see this poured out. It's called the sacrament of reconciliation. I remember my first experiences of it as though it were yesterday. I'd known various self-described "recovering Catholics" who loved to brag about how "guilty" confession made them feel. I never understood that, because I was raised completely outside the Church, and I could tell you all about guilt.

When I encountered the sacrament, it was a miracle (literally)! Imagine: a place where you could go and pour out all the poison of shame you had been lugging around for years. And when it was all over, you didn't get some psychoanalysis that provided nothing whatsoever to help. You didn't get somebody saying, "You sicken me! Get out of my sight!" You got a father putting his hands on your head and saying, with a voice like the waters of the sea washing your whole dead past away, "I absolve you of all your sins in the name of the Father, and of the Son, and of the Holy Spirit. Go in peace."

It didn't—couldn't—cost a thing, and it was the most precious thing in the world. And more than the forgiveness (which was enough!) was the fact that, for God, forgiveness was *not* enough. He insisted on pouring out grace so that, as I walked out of the confessional, I was not just forgiven but made stronger with his divine life to do better next time. He is proactive, that One. He forgives willingly, lavishly, not grudgingly. It is as if he loves me or something!

In this sacrament I saw not only God's forgiveness but also the tirelessness of our priests, modeling what the work of mercy looks like. I remember asking a couple of priests about what it felt like to sit there week after week, month after month, year after year, as the endless litany of human failure, wretchedness, and loss paraded in and out of that little box. I think, were it me, I would go crazy having to listen to the endless round of repetitive sins and moral wreckage. What, I wondered, must it be like to have to subject yourself to the torrent of sewage and, when you have heard it all yet again, to reply with mercy and a prayer of grace? I wonder if a priest ever feels awkward talking to people whose sins he knows all about.

One priest told me, to my amazement, that he never remembered a thing and was at perfect peace once he exited the confessional—a grace he chalked up to his ordination. That was striking. What was even more striking was that another priest said he found confession to be the most beautiful sacrament it was his honor to celebrate.

"People come in, and they are absolutely genuine," he said. "They tell the truth about their sins as best they can, and then, when the words of absolution are pronounced, they go out with the mask taken away and their own true face revealed."

It was a point he insisted on: that sin is the mask and Jesus Christ the true face of each person.

That truth lies behind the Church's insistence on forgiving sins willingly. Far too many of us (me included) think of forgiveness as "pretending a sin was not committed." It's closer to the mark to say that forgiveness is "realizing that sin does not name us, Christ does." Ever since God the Son joined himself to our fallen humanity, took it down to the grave with him, and raised it up all the way to the right hand of the Father in glory, he made himself, not our sin, the most fundamental fact about the human person. No matter how many sins we commit, we cannot pile them up high enough to touch him as he sits at the right hand of the Father in his glorified humanity. Even our murder of him had no power to stop his love for us: He instead made it the fountainhead of our race's greatest blessing. Now he, not our sin, is the last Word on who the human person is.

Because of this he has a toehold in even the darkest heart. That does not mean automatic heaven for one and all. It means that we can hand the sinner (sometimes an impenitent sinner) over to Jesus in the hope that he (who is closer to the sinner than we could ever hope to be) will transform fallen human nature with his divinized human nature. As we do that, we share a bit more in his divinized human nature and do something that is simply not possible apart from his Spirit: forgive offenses willingly.

CHAPTER 13

Comfort the Afflicted

*A*s I was writing this book, I got an earache. I don't mean a little twingy pain, like a headache or a sore toe. I mean Most Excruciating Pain I Have Felt in Three Decades. Up there with the Great Wisdom Tooth Agony of '78; worse than the Line Drive to the Groin of '69. We're talking debilitating anguish here, unable-to-function-or-think levels of pain. I didn't know it was possible to hurt that much from a simple infection to the ear canal. I will never forget it. It makes me marvel at how the human race could have maintained its sanity without ciprofloxacin, hydrocodone, and ibuprofen (all thanks be to God for these marvelous gifts!).

I mentioned my agonies on my blog (because sitting at a keyboard distracting myself from the eye-watering pain was less excruciating than lying down at five one morning). Lots of people replied with kind offers of prayer. And they did something else: Many shared, in addition to the home remedies and medical tips, their own stories of ear anguish to console me. It was all as natural as breathing—and curious when you think about it.

Why are we compelled, when we can do nothing else, to tell the afflicted of our afflictions? And why are we comforted by such tales? The fact that other people once howled in agony with *their* earaches should not, it would seem, make me feel any better. Indeed, by a certain logic, it should only make me feel worse—for them. But in fact, there *is* something comforting about knowing others have felt what we feel and, conversely, there is something offensive when those who have not been there presume to stoop down and tell us to buck up.

Of course, this sort of identity politics will get you only so far in dealing with suffering. Because at the end of the day, what actually healed my earache was not the empathy of fellow earache sufferers. It was a competent physician, who, while he may never have *felt* my pain, knew which drugs would kill the bacteria and *relieve* my pain.

That doesn't mean empathy is worthless. It means that there is more than one dimension to comforting the afflicted. Identifying with the sufferer is great. God did it when he sent his only begotten Son to identify with us in our sufferings. As Hebrews says:

> It was fitting that he, for whom and by whom all things exist, in bringing many sons to glory, should make the pioneer of their salvation perfect through suffering.... Therefore he had to be made like his brethren in every respect, so that he might become a merciful and faithful high priest in the service of God, to make expiation for the sins of the people. For because he himself has suffered and been tempted, he is able to help those who are tempted. (Hebrews 2:10, 17–18)

It is therefore priestly to let one's sufferings be a sort of mediating agent between the sufferings of Christ crucified and the sufferings of our neighbor. As St. Paul says, God "comforts us in all our affliction, so that we may be able to comfort those who are in any affliction, with the comfort with which we ourselves are comforted by God. For as we share abundantly in Christ's sufferings, so through Christ we share abundantly in comfort too. If we are afflicted, it is for your comfort and salvation; and if we are comforted, it is for your comfort, which you experience when you patiently endure the same sufferings that we suffer" (2 Corinthians 1:4–6).

But there is also a danger here. For we can take our status as victims, disconnect it from Christ crucified, and turn it into the source of our identity. When we do that, we become idolaters and quickly descend into a particularly silly sort of sin that grants only members of the approved victim class any right to speak to matters affecting the common good. So some claim that only women can address abortion, only soldiers can discuss war, only gay people can discuss gay marriage, only terminally ill people can address euthanasia, and the like.

This is nonsense. When I get treatment for an earache, I don't want somebody who once had an earache to treat me. I want somebody who knows how to treat an earache. When we want to rightly order human society, we should consult with the human race about the common good, because the common good is *common* and affects us all, not only the approved victims. Moreover, we want to hear from those with the relevant knowledge, not merely from grievance groups with parochial agendas. We look to *tradition* and, more than that, sacred tradition, because it gives God's perspective as well as that of millions of ordinary people down through the ages in what Chesterton aptly called "the democracy of the dead."

This is part of the genius of the Catholic tradition in comforting the afflicted. On the one hand, it's comforting to hear from fellow victims, living and dead. If that cloud of witnesses could make it, so can you. It is even more comforting to know that God the Son endured the worst suffering and won through to the Resurrection, promising that same grace and power to us, if we will remain in him. But here's the paradox: The other part of the gospel's comfort is the strange doctrine that God the Father is "impassible." That is, he is *not* subject to suffering or affliction and *cannot* be moved by the emotions that move us.

That seems problematic. Doesn't it contradict what I just said about the bureaucrat without experience sitting in a far-off room? Strangely, no. Because comfort comes from knowing not merely that others have suffered as you have but that they have come through their suffering to the place where "the dwelling of God is with men. He will dwell with them, and they shall be his people, and God himself will be with them; he will wipe away every tear from their eyes, and death shall be no more, neither shall there be mourning nor crying nor pain any more, for the former things have passed away" (Revelation 21:3–4). In our affliction, what we want is not only to have somebody suffering beside us but to know that there is someplace where all this pain and horror lose their power. Sam Gamgee is a comfort to Frodo in his affliction because, like Christ, he stands beside him and even carries him in the struggle across the Plains of

Gorgoroth and up the purgatorial slopes of Mount Doom. But Sam's comfort comes when, like Christ, he casts his gaze on the place where the troubles of this world cannot reach:

> Far above the Ephel Duath in the West the night-sky was still dim and pale. There, peeping among the cloud-wrack above a dark tor high up in the mountains, Sam saw a white star twinkle for a while. The beauty of it smote his heart, as he looked up out of the forsaken land, and hope returned to him. For like a shaft, clear and cold, the thought pierced him that in the end the Shadow was only a small and passing thing: there was light and high beauty forever beyond its reach.[1]

The good news of the "impassibility" of God is like that. There is a perfect happiness in God that the devil cannot ever harm or even touch. To be sure, God incarnate "was wounded for our transgressions, / he was bruised for our iniquities; / upon him was the chastisement that made us whole, / and with his stripes we are healed" (Isaiah 53:5). Yet the miracle of the thing is that it was for the joy that was set before him—the joy of the impassible Father who is pure happiness—that Jesus endured the cross, despising the shame, and now he is seated at the right hand of the throne of God (see Hebrews 12:2).

Something in our nature conforms to this. We are comforted in our affliction by shared suffering. But we require as well the anchor of hope that there is, somewhere, a place far above the cloud-wrack where we shall find the joy that is not—and cannot be—touched by the suffering we face here. It is exactly that paradox that moves St. Paul to remind us, "I consider that the sufferings of this present time are not worth comparing with the glory that is to be revealed to us" (Romans 8:18).

Of course, there are many kinds of affliction, and all the corporal works of mercy, from feeding the hungry to burying the dead, aim to relieve them. But this begs the question: Why a separate work of mercy that seems to recapitulate all these others?

I think the secret lies in the fact that comforting the afflicted is a *spiritual* work of mercy. This makes exactly Jesus' point in countering the devil (and the entire naturalistic bent of the present age): Man shall not live by bread alone but by every word that proceeds from the mouth of God (see Matthew 4:4). The deepest affliction is not, in the end, bodily but spiritual. We can endure incredible physical hardship if we are secure in the love of God, the grace of Jesus Christ, and the hope of heaven. This has been demonstrated countless times in the crucible of human history and the laboratory of the saints. Conversely, as the suicide of every rich, famous, powerful, or glamorous person attests, a material world filled with everything the devil offers is, in the end, weary, stale, flat, and unprofitable apart from God.

The sleek, fat, and wealthy Citizen Kane, alone and tormented in spirit, is more afflicted than a man who has lost both his legs but who remains secure in the love of Christ crucified. He requires a comfort that nothing in this world can supply. And his doom, should he refuse repentance, is to become a thing no such comfort will ever reach. This is one of the reasons that the hard task of the Comforter known as the Holy Spirit is often to afflict the comfortable before comforting the afflicted. From Saul of Tarsus to Hans Frank to Charles Colson to Karla Faye Tucker, the Christian tradition is chockablock with men and women who were supremely secure in their pride and who needed to be painfully taken apart down to their foundations in order to be rebuilt by God.

Indeed, in them we are only seeing the truth about ourselves. For we who may not have committed sins so grave that our fall was shattering are nonetheless creatures whose redemption requires nothing less than the horror of Golgotha. That God has favored us with the grace of a quiet life is due entirely to his grace, not because we are just better and nicer than others. There but for the grace of God go we.

That said, the subject here is the comforting of the afflicted, not the admonishing of sinners. There is something in us called "cowardice" that sometimes prefers to admonish the afflicted and comfort the sinner, especially the wealthy and powerful sinner. Everybody's seen it. It's the sort of mentality that tells the grieving child she wouldn't have lost her dolly if she weren't so irresponsible. It's the mentality of the Holocaust denier who says, "It never happened, and besides, the Jews deserved it." It's seen in the pundit uttering weepy excuses for the rich men who offered free toasters to uneducated people while fast-talking them into that unsustainable home loan, all the while excoriating the poor who thought the banks knew what they were doing.

Of course, this brings us to a tricky question: namely, who are the afflicted, and who is their neighbor? Jesus answered this question for all time in one of his most outrageously offensive parables. The reason it doesn't offend *us* is that we no longer share the tribal affiliations, historical grievances, and hostilities of his audience. Retold, in modern terms, it would go something like this:

> And behold, a lawyer stood up to put him to the test, saying, "Teacher, what shall I do to inherit eternal life?" He said to him, "What is written in the law? How do you read it?" And he answered, "You shall love the Lord your God with all your heart, and with all your soul, and with all your strength, and with all your mind; and your neighbor as yourself." And he said to him, "You have answered right; do this, and you will live." But he, desiring to justify himself, said to Jesus, "And who is my neighbor?" Jesus replied, "An American medical worker was going down from Kabul to the Afghan–Iranian border, and he fell among al Qaida, who stripped him and beat him, and departed, leaving him half dead. Now by chance an American military contractor was going down that road; and when he saw him he passed by on the other side. So likewise two congressmen on a fact-finding mission, one a Democrat and the other a Republican, when they came to the place and saw him, passed by on the other side. But a member of the Taliban, as he journeyed, came to where he was; and when he saw him, he had compassion, and went to him and bound up his wounds, pouring on oil and wine; then he set him on his own beast and brought him to an inn, and took care of him. And the next day he took out fifty American dollars and gave them to the innkeeper, saying, 'Take care of him; and whatever more you spend, I will repay you when I come

back.' Which of these three, do you think, proved neighbor
to the man who fell among the robbers?" He said, "The one
who showed mercy on him." And Jesus said to him, "Go and
do likewise." (Luke 10:25–37, *Revised Shea Paraphrase*)

The Jews to whom Jesus spoke had every bit as much reason to hate
Samaritans as Americans have to hate the Taliban. The bitter ethnic
and religious loathing ran deep, with real stories of real outrages
committed against Jews, just as we have suffered real outrages committed by the Taliban.[2] And yet Jesus overlooks the many examples
of heroic goodness in Israel's history and the many real sins and evils
of the Samaritans and constructs *this* story in order to make his
point. Why?

Precisely because his purpose is nothing less than to reveal the radically catholic nature of his mission. He's not kidding when he tells
us his project of redemption is to extend to the whole world. He's not
kidding when he commands us to look past the easy labels and shib-
boleths and tribal identity badges and recognize that not only are we
capable of evil as great as that of Saul of Tarsus, Hans Frank, and
Karla Faye Tucker but that those whom we have assumed to be irre-
deemable animals are capable of responding to grace. In a word, that
our neighbor is every person we meet.

The Church's historic response to affliction of both body and soul
is notoriously indiscriminate and profligate. From the medieval tradition of sanctuary (which protected people from mob violence) to
the invention of the hospital and the establishment of the greatest
system of charitable works on the planet, to the massive impact of
Mother Teresa's care for the poorest of the poor, and, of course, in the

miracle of the sacraments of confession and anointing, the relief of the afflictions of body and spirit has been the work of the Church down through the ages. All this, true, is compounded with the reality of sin, so that many afflictions have been *caused* by sinful Christians as well as alleviated by them. But the tradition remains what it is, however well or poorly we carry it out.

Nor is comforting the afflicted the exclusive property of the Judeo-Christian tradition. As Jesus' Good Samaritan illustrates, it is not a work limited to the visible members of the Church. This is a sign of hope, because it illuminates the fact that our obedience to the Spirit is not in our yakety-yak but in our *obedience* to Christ.

Meanwhile, the main task is not to peer into the soul of our neighbor and speculate about what his verdict might be at the Judgment. Rather, it is to mind our own business and comfort the afflicted as best we can. Unhappily, these are not hard to find. "The mass of men," said Thoreau, "lead lives of quiet desperation."[3] Begin wherever you are and you can scarcely avoid running into all manner of affliction of body and soul. How to comfort the sufferer? All that we have just considered points the way.

Comforting the afflicted is the work of the king, prophet, and priest you and I became by virtue of our baptism. The corporal works of mercy are the key if the affliction is physical. In this we see the kingly office exercised to prudently order the world and its resources—food, medicine, shelter; physical, emotional, social, spiritual care—in the service of human need. But we must also remember that man does not live by bread alone. The prophet speaks to that, sometimes in encouragement and sometimes in rebuke (especially to idolatrous comforts such as drugs, money, sex, and power). But in particular, our task is priestly in that we stand with the sufferer as Christ crucified stands with us. We emphasize the compassion—the "suffering with"—of God the Son. But we also point to God the impassible Father, the star far above the cloud-wrack enshrouding this world of pain. We remind the afflicted of the hope and joy untouchable by all the pain Satan can throw at us—and that it will be ours in Christ Jesus.

In the end, this means that comforting the afflicted is rooted in the holy sacrifice of the Mass. For that is where our kingly, prophetic, and priestly office finds its deepest source and fulfillment. When we pray for the afflicted, we bear them to God the impassible Father via Christ crucified. When we receive the Eucharist and are sent as living tabernacles into the world, we bear nothing less than the hope of heaven to every sufferer. We may not see how or whether that grace comes to fruition, but the reality and power are there in Christ Jesus, fully present in the Eucharist.

CHAPTER 14

Pray for the Living and the Dead

ONE OF THE SILLIER JOKES told about Catholics is the one about the guy who gets ushered inside the pearly gates by St. Peter. As Pete shows him around the Elysian fields, they pass by a little gothic structure and hear voices praying in Latin.

"Shh!" says Peter and leads the new arrival tiptoe past the little building.

Out of earshot, the new arrival turns to Peter and says, "What's up with those guys?"

Peter says, "Those are the Catholics. They think they're the only ones here."

Some laugh. But truth to tell, that's a completely false view of average Catholic piety and prayer. The Church is, in fact, wildly promiscuous with its prayer life. *Everybody* gets prayed for by the Catholic Church. Sooner or later, after mentioning all those people you always pray for as an ordinary Catholic—family, friends, enemies, people from the office and church, that guy who cut you off on the freeway this morning, the pope, bishops, priests, favorite religious, politicians, movie stars in embarrassing situations, athletes, rock stars, and sundry media types—you then go on and cover all the bases you might normally miss (Hitler, Osama bin Laden, that wino you remember seeing when you were twelve) with the great all-purpose prayer "for all those who have no one to pray for them." And if you don't get around to it as a layperson in your daily devotions, there's always the liturgy during the Triduum, when everyone with and without a pulse gets a mention before the throne of grace. There's a huge generosity of spirit there that roughly corresponds to the great pagan Greek impulse of cautious piety. The ancients prayed to the Unknown God; we pray for the Unknown Sinner.

That's the first thing that sticks out when we look at Catholics at prayer. It's a phenomenon that reminds me of Chesterton's remarks about the supposed contrast between "gentle Jesus" and the "harsh, forbidding Church." He wrote:

> We have all heard people say a hundred times over, for they seem never to tire of saying it, that the Jesus of the New Testament is indeed a most merciful and humane lover of humanity, but that the Church has hidden this human character in repellent dogmas and stiffened it with ecclesiastical terrors till it has taken on an inhuman character. This is, I venture to repeat, very nearly the reverse of the truth. The truth is that it is the image of Christ in the churches that is almost entirely mild and merciful. It is the image of Christ in the Gospels that is a good many other things as well. The figure in the Gospels does indeed utter in words of almost heart-breaking beauty his pity for our broken hearts. But they are very far from being the only sort of words that he

utters. Nevertheless they are almost the only kind of words that the Church in its popular imagery ever represents him as uttering. That popular imagery is inspired by a perfectly sound popular instinct. The mass of the poor are broken, and the mass of the people are poor, and for the mass of mankind the main thing is to carry the conviction of the incredible compassion of God. But nobody with his eyes open can doubt that it is chiefly this idea of compassion that the popular machinery of the Church does seek to carry. The popular imagery carries a great deal to excess the sentiment of 'Gentle Jesus, meek and mild.' It is the first thing that the outsider feels and criticises in a Pieta or a shrine of the Sacred Heart. As I say, while the art may be insufficient, I am not sure that the instinct is unsound. In any case there is something appalling, something that makes the blood run cold, in the idea of having a statue of Christ in wrath. There is something insupportable even to the imagination in the idea of turning the corner of a street or coming out into the spaces of a marketplace, to meet the petrifying petrifaction of that figure as it turned upon a generation of vipers, or that face as it looked at the face of a hypocrite. The Church can reasonably be justified therefore if she turns the most merciful face or aspect towards men; but it is certainly the most merciful aspect that she does turn.[1]

So while our Lord is unafraid to remind his followers that sometimes you should not beat your head against a wall with some hardhearted enemy who won't listen and who only wants to destroy you ("Do not give dogs what is holy; and do not throw your pearls before swine, lest they trample them under foot and turn to attack you" [Matthew 7:6]), yet his Church is not especially eager to make that judgment call till the last possible minute. Similarly, while St. John (following his Master) tells us, "There is sin which is mortal; I do not say that one is to pray for that" (1 John 5:16), Catholics, still and all, have a long history of praying for those in a state of mortal sin anyway. So outsized is the Catholic instinct to keep hoping for the sinner to the bitter end that one early theologian, Origen, speculated that God's grace was so overwhelming that, in the end, even the devil himself would be saved.[2] The Church rejected that speculation, and my point here is not to reignite Origenism (I accept the church's teaching). Rather my point is that this impulse to pray for the worst of the worst is a deep structural feature in Catholic culture. Catholic prayer, both in liturgy and in popular piety, is marked by a stubborn refusal to refuse prayer for anybody—a refusal that finds its expression in the last of the spiritual works of mercy.

Witness the beautiful gush of quite sincere prayer for atheist provocateur Christopher Hitchens when he was diagnosed with esophageal cancer. I think the vast bulk of these prayers were basically motivated by ordinary human and Christian compassion. In my own case, a favorite priest friend of mine died of esophageal cancer, and it was painful to watch him slowly starve to death. So I prayed for Hitchens, as did a bunch of others, because that's what you *do*: pray for the living and the dead. Hitchens is alive. Good enough for me. Let's pray. We can quarrel with him when we're done. And such expressions of agenda-free charity do touch the heart—even

Hitchens's heart. As he said in an interview: "I have to say there's some extremely nice people ... who have said that I'm in their prayers, and I can only say that I'm touched by the thought."[3]

I tend to approach prayer not as a saint but as a manual laborer. It's a duty I feel, not especially a thing I like doing or feel competent at. On my blog I started getting sundry prayer requests from random readers and began posting them, largely because I feel inept as an intercessory pray-er. I hoped that maybe somebody out there in cyberspace might have the charism I lack in having a clue how to pray. I thought I was very clever fobbing this off on others, but I stupidly failed to foresee that this would inevitably result in lots more prayer requests. I continue to post them, along with my fumbling blather in the ear of the Almighty, advising him on how to proceed. I haven't the slightest idea whether my prayers do a lick of good for the person making the request. But I figure that if I mix my prayers in with those of others who are closer to the throne, then maybe they'll get lost in the pack and I'll look as if I know what I'm doing.

Also, I think such prayers, whatever they do for those requesting prayer, have done me good in simply building the discipline of prayer. I have found that, over time, I am not as prone to strategizing about earthly junk or giving in to the idea that there's no hope, but rather I focus on God.

One can always get all navel-gazey about this sort of thing, and sometimes motives are worth a look. After prayer for Hitchens went out, it was followed by lots of meta-analysis of motivation, with reverberations and recriminations. Of course there was some "How can you pray for him when he's so nastily atheistic?" and so on. Also we got the charge of showy piety. ("Look at me! I'm praying for my enemies!") And there was even the charge that it was a pious, church-lady way of saying, "Hey, Hitchens! Look at how superiorly loving I am to you and your angry atheist buddies!"

Understandable to a degree. The obligation to pray for one's enemies can put one in a bind. It *does* sound pretty church-ladyish to look at some guy who just finished reaming you out in a steroid rage and say, "God bless you," especially when the physiological fight-or-flight response leaves you trembling with animal passions you are trying to master by dint of will. To the onlooker you can often resemble a hypocrite in denial about his hatred when, in fact, you are laboring to do the right thing.

Moreover, you *can* find Pharisees who use prayer as a passive-aggressive weapon ("Have you heard about John Smith—that's S-M-I-T-H? Let me whisper the juicy details! So you can pray.")

And these are but a few of the ways that praying for the living can get you into trouble, whether real or perceived. But still, we are called to do it—indiscriminately and constantly. The world is dying for want of Christians actually living out the common priesthood of our baptism.

The essence of priesthood is twofold: It entails "standing between" and "offering sacrifice." We stand, as priests, between God and man. And the sacrifice we offer, as laypeople, is ourselves in union with Christ. So Paul tells us: "I appeal to you therefore, brethren, by the mercies of God, to present your bodies as a living sacrifice, holy and acceptable to God, which is your spiritual worship" (Romans 12:1).

Of course, what sanctifies our self-offering is not us but Jesus Christ, who offers his body and blood on the cross and to us in the sacrifice of the Mass. Because his body and blood are holy, our bodies are made holy and become part of the offering. And as they are offered in union with him, they participate in the work of salvation. That's why Paul can write one of the most Catholic passages in all of Scripture: "Now I rejoice in my sufferings for your sake, and in my flesh I complete what is lacking in Christ's afflictions for the sake of his body, that is, the church" (Colossians 1:24).

Paul's offering of his body (and our offering of ours) is incorporated into Christ's and becomes part of Christ's self-offering to the Father in each Mass. Our sufferings are joined to his, but also our prayers are joined to his. For as Paul tells us, we "yield [ourselves] to God as men who have been brought from death to life, and [our] members to God as instruments of righteousness" (Romans 6:13). That includes our tongues, which offer prayer for the living and the dead by the power of the Holy Spirit.

It's a bit of a toss-up which is harder: praying for the living or praying the dead. The problem with the living is that they stubbornly retain free will, so there is always the danger that, in the words of the Harvard Law of Animal Behavior, "People, under carefully controlled laboratory conditions, will do exactly as they please." Prayer for things like repentance, healing from addiction, relationships, and other such things can all go radically awry. People pray their guts out for things that never come to pass in this world and that can be heartbreaking to endure. Often such prayer can wind up being a journey of discovery. We think we know what's best only to discover that we were radically wrong—and that God's grace was changing *us*, not the circumstances we were demanding he fix. The grinding stone of other human wills can often be how God polishes us through our prayers.

On the other hand, prayer for the dead has its own challenges. For of course, the dead are unusually quiet about whether your prayers do them any good. Now and then blessed souls (like St. Perpetua) are favored with a vision of their dead kid brother turning up happy and healthy in the heavenlies after a Mass was said for him. But most of us don't seem to rate these aids to faith. Instead we go on the insistence of the Church that prayers for the dead, like prayers for the living, are not merely good and pious and consoling to *us* but *effective for the dead*.

For the truth is, we don't merely *remember* the dead by our prayers; we *help* them. In short, prayer for the dead is not about us. It's not some sort of self-hypnosis, therapy, or coping mechanism. It's about assisting the dead in the completion of their purgation, which, but for our prayers, they would be hard-pressed to complete themselves.

This cuts right to the heart of the mystery of the Incarnation: the reality of the body as the "hinge of salvation." What we have that the dead in purgatory lack is the same thing whereby God saved us: a body. Our body matters so much that God himself so created the universe that we could not be saved without his taking on a body like ours. And because he did that, the Son of God could speak of his death as a true necessity for our salvation, stating, "I have a baptism to be baptized with; and how I am constrained until it is accomplished!" (Luke 12:50), and even praying that the cup be taken from him "if it be possible" (Matthew 26:39).

It was not possible. Therefore the body is bound up with the saving power of God. And offering our bodies as living sacrifices in union with Christ's in the sacrifice of the Mass therefore becomes a powerful means by which we can pray for those who have died, helping them on their way to full conformity to Christ. That's why the tradition has always linked prayer with fasting and other forms of penance—particularly on behalf of the dead.

Some have difficulty with this, though it is difficult to see why. If we can pray for each other—if, in fact, we are *commanded* to pray for each other—it's hard to see why we shouldn't pray for those who have died. The practice predates the establishment of the Church (see 2 Maccabees 12:38–46), follows from the logic of all prayer (by which creatures are made free participants in Christ's saving work), and has no internal contradiction to it. Since we are members of one another (see Romans 12:5) and neither life nor death can sever us from the love of God in Christ (see Romans 8:38–39), then our prayers can extend beyond the grave to benefit those who are still in the process of becoming fully conformed to the image and likeness of Christ. About the only objection you can make is that the dead, being dead, are past probation and so their choice for heaven or hell has been decided at death.

True enough. But what do we know about that? Zilch. What we know is that Christ said to pray for God's will to be done and for his kingdom to come. So we pray that Joe the mechanic, who was a decent enough guy and who didn't rip you off when your alternator broke, will be met with favor in the Great Assizes because the King will say to him, "My alternator was busted, and you didn't rip me off.

Inasmuch as you did it to the least of these, you did it to me." You pray for that kid who gave you swirlies in junior high, that maybe in the years afterward his three divorces and drug-addicted kids helped buff off whatever made him the nasty kid you remember and gave him, in the end, the bitterly won gift of humility. You step on to an airplane that your father helped Boeing build and remember to pray, yet again, for the repose of his soul, grateful for the countless gifts he gave you.

In the end, of course, you often don't know what your prayers are doing for those folks in the beyond. But you know God. And you know that Jesus wants them in heaven even more than you do. You know that while you have never endured the extremity of crucifixion for them, Jesus has. And so you pray in hope, not that your prayers are such hot stuff that God just has to listen in his awe of you, but that when they are joined to Christ's prayers remarkable things can happen, as they have happened down through the centuries when people stop speculating about prayer and begin doing it.

What Next?

A book on the corporal and spiritual works of mercy can't be complete if I leave the reader merely to close it and murmur, "That was a nice reflection."

St. James is direct:

> But be doers of the word, and not hearers only, deceiving your-selves. For if any one is a hearer of the word and not a doer, he is like a man who observes his natural face in a mirror; for he observes himself and goes away and at once forgets what he was like. But he who looks into the perfect law, the law of lib-erty, and perseveres, being no hearer that forgets but a doer that acts, he shall be blessed in his doing. (James 1:22–25)

To that end, permit me to give you before we part, gentle reader, some possible places to turn to in order to put legs on the things we have been discussing here. The idea is not so much that you rush about doing all fourteen of the works of mercy. I certainly don't, nor does anybody else— including Jesus while he was on earth. It is for the body of Christ and her many members to see to it that all the works of mercy are performed (see 1 Corinthians 12; Romans 12). But by the same token, it is because we are members of the body of Christ (I assume the reader is baptized) that we are obligated to start somewhere to attempt the works of mercy. Here, then, are just a few possible starting places for living out or supporting the works of mercy.

Feed the Hungry

Mercy Corps helps people in the world's toughest places turn the crises of natural disaster, poverty, and conflict into opportunities for progress. Driven by local needs and market conditions, their programs provide communities with the tools and support they need to transform their own lives. Their worldwide team of 3,700 professionals is improving the lives of 16.7 million people in more than forty countries.

Mercy Corps
P.O. Box 2669, Dept. W
Portland, OR 97208-2669
Phone: 888-256-1900
Website: www.mercycorps.org

Food for the Poor is the third-largest international relief and development charity in the United States, feeding two million poor every day. Its Christian relief programs and projects are helping children and the poorest of the poor by providing food, housing, health care, education, water projects, emergency relief, and micro-enterprise assistance in the Caribbean and Latin America.

Food for the Poor
6401 Lyons Road
Coconut Creek, FL 33073
Phone: 954-427-2222 or 800-427-9104
Website: www.foodforthepoor.org

Feed the Children has, over three decades, grown into one of the world's largest private organizations dedicated to helping hungry and hurting people, shipping millions of pounds of food and other essentials to children and families in all 50 states and in 34 foreign countries, supplementing more than 760,000 meals a day worldwide and reaching out to help children and families in 119 countries around the globe.

Feed the Children
P.O. Box 36
Oklahoma City, OK 73101
Phone: 800-627-4556
Website: www.feedthechildren.org

Give Drink to the Thirsty

Global Water was founded in 1982, by former U.S. ambassador John McDonald and Dr. Peter Bourne, to help save the lives of people in developing countries affected by unclean water. Rather than providing short-term supplies like food and bottled water, Global Water focuses on permanent solutions to a region's water needs.

Global Water
Project Management Office
3600 S. Harbor Blvd., Suite 514
Oxnard, CA 93035
Phone: 805-985-3057
Website: www.globalwater.org

H2OAfrica's objective is to increase awareness of the African situation, empower people to take action, and create sustainable alliances between people who want to help, the best organizations in the field to make it happen, and some of the communities of Africa that have no clean water.

Water.org
920 Main Street, Suite 1800
Kansas City, MO 64105
Phone: 816-877-8400
Website: www.water.org

Drop in the Bucket has constructed more than eighty wells and a number of sanitation systems at locations in Tanzania, Mozambique, South Sudan, Chad, Kenya, and Uganda.

Drop in the Bucket
P.O. Box 3697
Los Angeles, CA 90078
Website: www.dropinthebucket.org

Clothe the Naked

The **Salvation Army** is always happy to take your donations of clothing.

Contact this organization either by checking the local phone directory or by going to www.salvationarmyusa.org and searching by zip code for your local Salvation Army location.

The **Society of St. Vincent de Paul** helps the poor with needs, especially clothing.

Check the local phone directory for one of its local ministries, or contact the national office:

National Council of the United States
Society of St. Vincent de Paul

58 Progress Parkway
St. Louis, MO 63043-3706
Phone: 314-576-3993
Website: www.svdpusa.org

Catholic Relief Services carries out the commitment of the bishops of the United States to assist the poor and vulnerable overseas. It is motivated by the gospel of Jesus Christ to cherish, preserve, and uphold the sacredness and dignity of all human life, foster charity and justice, and embody Catholic social and moral teaching.

Catholic Relief Services
228 W. Lexington Street
Baltimore, MD 21201-3413
Phone: 888-277-7575 or 800-736-3467
Website: www.crs.org

Harbor the Harborless

Seattle's **Union Gospel Mission**'s self-description says it all: "To serve, rescue, and transform those in greatest need through the grace of Jesus Christ." And it's been doing it for nearly eighty years.

Union Gospel Mission
P.O. Box 202
Seattle, WA 98111-0202
Phone: 206-723-0767
Website: www.ugm.org

Incorporated in 1972, **Covenant House** has been leading the effort to help homeless kids. Today it is the largest privately funded agency in the

Americas that provides food, shelter, immediate crisis care, and an array of other important services to homeless, throwaway, and runaway kids. Covenant House doesn't stop at offering an immediate safe harbor for homeless youth; it strives to move each kid forward down the path to an independent adulthood, free from the risk of future homelessness.

Covenant House
460 West 41 Street
New York, NY 10036-6801
Phone: 212-613-0300
Website: www.covenanthouse.org

Sheltersforwomen.org has information on shelters for battered women, families, youth, homeless people, and drug addicts in your local community. It provides links that help get people back on their feet.

Visit the Sick

The **Hospice Volunteer Association** is a diverse, well-trained, and globally unbounded volunteer community with a shared commitment to provide the most compassionate service possible to those who are dying and their bereaved.

Phone: 866-489-4325
Website: www.hospicevolunteerassociation.org/default.aspx

Ronald McDonald Houses provide a "home away from home" for families so they can stay close by their hospitalized child at little or no cost. They are built on the simple idea that nothing else should matter when a family is focused on healing their child—not where they can afford to stay, where they will get their next meal, or where they will lay their heads at night.

Ronald McDonald House Charities
One Kroc Drive
Oak Brook, IL 60523
Phone: 630-623-7048
Website: http://rmhc.org

Consult with your **parish or diocese** to see what opportunities there might be for you to minister to the sick, elderly, or shut-in in your area.

Ransom the Captive

Anti-Slavery International works at local, national, and international levels to eliminate all forms of slavery around the world.

Anti-Slavery International
Thomas Clarkson House
The Stableyard
Broomgrove Road
London SW9 9TL
U.K.
Phone: 011[from USA] +44 (0)20 7501 8920
Website: www.antislavery.org

The **Not For Sale Campaign** equips and mobilizes smart activists to deploy innovative solutions to reabolish slavery in their own backyards and across the globe.

Not For Sale
270 Capistrano Road, Suite 2
Half Moon Bay, CA 94019
Phone: 650-560-9990
Website: www.notforsalecampaign.org

International Justice Mission is a human-rights agency that secures justice for victims of slavery, sexual exploitation, and other forms of violent oppression. IJM lawyers, investigators, and aftercare professionals work with local officials to ensure immediate victim rescue and aftercare, to prosecute perpetrators, and to promote functioning public justice systems.

International Justice Mission
P.O. Box 58147
Washington, D.C. 20037
Phone: 703-465-5495
Website: www.ijm.org

Bury the Dead

In addition to helping the living, relief agencies like **World Vision** also help to bury the dead after disasters like the earthquake in Haiti.

World Vision
P.O. Box 9716
Federal Way, WA 98063-9716
Phone: 888-511-6443
Website: www.worldvision.org

Reverence for the body is an extension of the reverence for life. **The Patients Rights Council** exists to support each person's right to die a natural death in an environment of love without being murdered by a culture eager to dispose of the weak and inconvenient.

The Patients Rights Council
P.O. Box 760
Steubenville, OH 43952

Phone: 740-282-3810 or 800-958-5678

Website: www.internationaltaskforce.org

The **Catholic Funeral Plan** is a guide to planning funerals that clearly explains what to do.

Phone: 877-886-7526

Website: www.cfppgh.com

Instruct the Ignorant

Christendom College is a Catholic coeducational college institutionally committed to the magisterium of the Roman Catholic Church. It provides a Catholic liberal-arts education, including an integrated core curriculum grounded in natural and revealed truth, the purpose of which at both the undergraduate and graduate levels is to form the whole person for a life spent in the pursuit of truth and wisdom. Intrinsic to such an education are the formation of moral character and the fostering of the spiritual life. This education prepares students for their role as faithful, informed, and articulate members of society and Christ's Church.

Christendom College

134 Christendom Drive

Front Royal, VA 22630

Phone: 800-877-5456

Website: www.christendom.edu

The **Holy Child Program** is a service of the Bethlehem Holy Child Program Corporation. It provides an intense alternative education and a program of therapeutic day treatment for children in the Bethlehem region in the Holy Land who suffer from untreated, complex mental-health issues and exposure to intergenerational trauma.

Children of Peace Foundation
P.O. Box 55148
Seattle, WA 98155 USA
Phone: 206-733-0911
Website: www.childrenofpeacefoundation.org

Trinity Formation Resources is a nonprofit ministry dedicated to helping Catholics understand, live, and share their Catholic faith.

Trinity Formation Resources
P.O. Box 24886
Federal Way, WA 98093
Phone: 253-835-5016 or 888-765-9269
Website: www.mycatholicfaith.org

Counsel the Doubtful

Catholic Answers is one of the nation's largest lay-run apostolates of Catholic apologetics and evangelization, dedicated to serving Christ by bringing the fullness of Catholic truth to the world. Catholic Answers helps good Catholics become better Catholics, brings former Catholics "home," and leads non-Catholics into the fullness of the faith.

Catholic Answers
2020 Gillespie Way
El Cajon, CA 92020
Phone: 619-387-7200
Website: www.catholic.com

Patrick Madrid offers all sorts of materials and seminars on Catholic faith that will strengthen those struggling with doubt.

Patrick Madrid
P.O. Box 640
Granville, OH 43023
Phone: 740-345-2705
Website: www.surprisedbytruth.com/

The **Pastoral Solutions Institute** helps those who are struggling with doubts about their marriage and their family. It strengthens husbands, wives, parents, and children to better live out the vocation of the domestic church.

Phone: 740-266-6461
Website: www.exceptionalmarriages.com

Admonish the Sinner

Bread for the World members write personal letters and e-mails and meet with members of Congress. Working through churches, campuses, and other organizations, they engage people in advocacy. Each year Bread for the World invites churches across the country to take up a nationwide Offering of Letters to Congress on an issue that is important to hungry and poor people. Together they build the political commitment needed to overcome hunger and poverty.

Bread for the World
425 Third Street SW, Suite 1200
Washington, D.C. 20024
Phone: 202-639-9400 or 800-822-7323
Website: www.bread.org

American Life League is the largest grassroots Catholic pro-life education organization in the United States. ALL is committed to the protection of all innocent human beings from the moment of creation to natural death. It is rooted in pro-life integrity that stands up for every innocent human being whose life is threatened by what Pope John Paul II called "the culture of death." That ranges from the single-cell human embryo to the elderly, the infirm, and others at risk of having their life terminated by acts of euthanasia.

American Life League
P.O. Box 1350
Stafford, VA 22555
Phone: 540-659-4171
Website: www.all.org

The purpose of the **Catholic Peace Fellowship** is to support Catholic conscientious objectors through education, counseling, and advocacy. Guided by a personalist philosophy, the CPF seeks to resist war by helping, one person at a time, those who choose not to participate in it.

Catholic Peace Fellowship
P.O. Box 4232
South Bend, IN 46634
Phone: 574-232-2811
Website: www.catholicpeacefellowship.org

Bear Wrongs Patiently

The **Third Order Regular Franciscans** are a penitential order dating back to the thirteenth century. They seek to do penance in the spirit of St. Francis.

Convento Dei SS. Cosma e Damiano
Via Dei Vori Imperiali 1

00186 Rome, Italy

Phone: 011[from USA] 39-066920441

Website: www.francescanitor.org/archive/porta.html

Retrouvaille is a program offering tools needed to rediscover a loving marriage relationship. Thousands of couples headed for cold, unloving relationships or divorce have successfully overcome their marriage problems by attending the program.

Phone: 800-470-2230

Find the Retrouvaille community closest to you at www.retrouvaille.org.

Another way of bearing wrongs patiently is to do it for others in your private life via the traditional penitential practices of **prayer, fasting, and almsgiving**. Try making a study (and a practice) of Jesus' counsel, in the Sermon on the Mount (see Matthew 6:1–18), about how to do these three things.

Forgive Offenses Willingly

The **sacrament of reconciliation** is the best means for living this work of mercy. Seek it at your parish, and bring to Jesus any sins you harbor against anybody, including yourself.

Rachel's Vineyard is a safe place to renew, rebuild, and redeem hearts broken by abortion. Weekend retreats offer a supportive, confidential, and nonjudgmental environment where women and men can express, release, and reconcile painful postabortive emotions to begin the process of restoration, renewal, and healing.

Rachel's Vineyard Ministries
808 N. Henderson Road., 2nd Floor
King of Prussia, PA 19406
Phone: 610-354-0555
Website: www.rachelsvineyard.org/

Immaculée Ilibagiza's **Left to Tell Charitable Fund** was founded to give homes, hope, and healing not only to children who survived the Rwandan genocide but to all the children of Africa.

Left to Tell Charitable Fund
c/o Hay House, Inc.
P.O. Box 5100
Carlsbad, CA 92018-5100
Websites: www.lefttotell.com/fund/index.php
www.immaculee.com/charity

Comfort the Afflicted

Doctors Without Borders / Médecins Sans Frontières (MSF) is an international medical humanitarian organization created in 1971 by doctors and journalists in France. Today MSF provides aid in nearly sixty countries to people whose survival is threatened by violence, neglect, or catastrophe due primarily to armed conflict, epidemics, malnutrition, natural disasters, or exclusion from health care. MSF provides independent, impartial assistance to those most in need. MSF reserves the right to speak out to bring attention to neglected crises, to challenge inadequacies or abuse of the aid system, and to advocate for improved medical treatments and protocols. In 1999 MSF received the Nobel Peace Prize.

Doctors Without Borders
333 7th Avenue, 2nd Floor
New York, NY 10001-5004
Phone: 212-679-6800
Website: www.doctorswithoutborders.org

The **Missionaries of Charity** are a religious order established in 1950 by Mother Teresa of Calcutta. They consist of more than 4,500 sisters and are active in 133 countries. Members of the order adhere to the vows of chastity, poverty, and obedience and to a fourth vow, to give "wholehearted and free service to the poorest of the poor."

Mother Teresa Centre
Piazza S. Gregorio al Celio, 2
00184 Rome, Italy
Phone: 011 [from USA] +39 06-772-60230
Website: www.motherteresa.org

Rooted in the healing ministry of Jesus, **Catholic Medical Mission Board** works collaboratively to provide quality health-care programs and services, without discrimination, to people in need around the world.

Catholic Medical Mission Board
10 West 17th Street
New York, NY 10011-5765
Phone: 212-242-7757 or 800-678-5659
Website: www.cmmb.org

Pray for the Living and the Dead

The **Franciscan Friars of the Atonement–Graymoor** have been praying for the living and the dead since 1898.

Franciscan Friars of the Atonement–Graymoor
1350 Route 9
P.O. Box 300
Garrison, NY 10524
Phone: 845-424-3671
Website: www.atonementfriars.org

The Institute for Christian Ministries (ICM) offers an ecumenical program of spiritual formation and training for healing ministry. Taught from a Catholic Christian perspective, Formation for Healing Ministry (FHM) is designed for use by Christian communities of all traditions.

Institute for Christian Ministries
2551 NE 205th Street
Shoreline, WA 98155-1431
Phone: 206-363-4394
Website: www.healingministry.org

Contact your **local diocese or parish** to get involved with a local ministry of intercessory prayer on behalf of the living and the dead.

Introduction to the Corporal and Spiritual Works of Mercy

1. Martin Luther, *Works*, vol. 48 (Minneapolis: Fortress, 1963), pp. 281–282.
2. John of the Cross, *Dichos* 64.
3. Gerard Manley Hopkins, "As Kingfishers Catch Fire."
4. Charles Chaput, "Catholic Charities USA, Homily at Red Rock," http://archden.org.

Chapter 1: Feed the Hungry

1. Paul Ehrlich, *The Population Bomb* (Cutchogue, N.Y.: Buccaneer, 1995), p. xi. Please note that the latter prophecy was removed from the 1971 edition of *The Population Bomb*, "as the food situation in India suddenly improved" (as noted in the Wikipedia article "The Population Bomb: Predictions").
2. Maslow's pyramid: a hierarchy of human needs proposed by psychologist Abraham Maslow in 1943, beginning with basic bodily needs, such as food and water, and moving on to include safety and emotional, psychological, social, and creative needs.
3. *Catechism of the Catholic Church* 2446; "Not to enable..." is from St. John Chrysostom, *Hom. in Lazaro* 2, 5: PG 48, 992; "The demands of justice..." is from *Apostolicam Auctuositatem* 8 §5; "When we attend..." is from St. Gregory the Great, *Regula Pastoralis.* 3, 21: PL 77, 87.
4. If you are stumped about a place to begin lending a hand, see the afterword of this book.

Chapter 2: Give Drink to the Thirsty

1. William Wyler directed the movie *Ben Hur* starring Charlton Heston.

Chapter 3: Clothe the Naked

1. Rite for the Baptism of One Child, May 15, 1969 (1970 Missal).
2. Sara Kaufman, "Following in Beyoncé's 'Single Ladies' Footsteps Strips 7-Year-Olds of Innocence," *Washington Post* (www.washingtonpost.com), May 15, 2010.

Chapter 5: Visit the Sick

1. Mary O'Driscoll, *Catherine of Siena: Passion for the Truth—Compassion for Humanity* (Hyde Park, N.Y.: New City, 2005), pp. 41–42.
2. Malcolm Muggeridge, *Something Beautiful for God: Mother Teresa of Calcutta* (New York: Harper and Row, 1971), p. 28.

Chapter 6: Ransom the Captive

1. Victor Hugo, *Les Miserables* (New York: Signet Classics, 1987).
2. C.S. Lewis, *The Great Divorce* (New York: HarperCollins, 2000), p. 28.

Chapter 7: Bury the Dead

1. Jennie Rothenberg Gritz, "Transcending God," *Atlantic* (www.theatlantic.com), July 2007.

Chapter 8: Instruct the Ignorant

1. G.K. Chesterton, *Heretics* (New York: John Lane, 1905), p. 67.

Chapter 9: Counsel the Doubtful

1. John Dominic Crossan, *Jesus: A Revolutionary Biography* (New York: HarperCollins, 1994), p. 154.
2. Interview with Dotson Rader, "There's a Lot of Hate in the World," *Parade* magazine (www.parade.com), February 17, 2010.
3. "When we've finally gotten serious about global warming, when the impacts are really hitting us and we're in a full worldwide scramble to minimize the damage, we should have war crimes trials for these bastards—some sort of climate Nuremberg." David Roberts, "The Denial Industry: An Excerpt from a New Book by George Monbiot," *Grist* magazine (www.grist.org), September 19, 2006.
4. "Cardinal Ratzinger Says Unilateral Attack on Iraq Not Justified," Zenit (www.zenit.org), September 22, 2002.
5. Thomas Aquinas, *Summa Theologiae*, I, q.4, art.3, reply to objection 4.
6. G.K. Chesterton, *Autobiography*, vol. 16 of *Collected Works* (San Francisco: Ignatius, 1988), p. 212.
7. C.S. Lewis, *The Magician's Nephew* (New York: HarperCollins, 1998), p. 72.
8. C.S. Lewis, *The Screwtape Letters* (New York: HarperCollins, 2001), pp. 138–139.
9. John Henry Newman, *Apologia Pro Vita Sua* (London: Longman, 1878), p. 239.

Chapter 10: Admonish the Sinner
1. For details of this case, go to www.courthousenews.com.
2. See Matthew Alexander and John Bruning, *How to Break a Terrorist: The U.S. Interrogators Who Used Brains, Not Brutality, to Take Down the Deadliest Man in Iraq* (New York: Free Press, 2008).
3. Anita Singh, "Richard Curtis and an Explosion of Publicity," *Daily Telegraph*, October 2, 2010, archived at www.telegraph.co.uk.

Chapter 12: Forgive Offenses Willingly
1. C.S. Lewis, *The Complete C.S. Lewis: Signature Classics* (New York: HarperCollins, 2002), p. 112.
2. Athanasius, *De Incarnatione* 54, 3: PG 25, 192B.

Chapter 13: Comfort the Afflicted
1. J.R.R. Tolkien, *The Return of the King: Being the Third Part of The Lord of the Rings* (New York: Random House, 2001), p. 211.
2. See, for instance, the book of Nehemiah, in which we see Samaritans engaged in a struggle to try to keep the Jewish people from rebuilding their holiest edifice, the temple.
3. Henry David Thoreau, *Walden* (Boston: Beacon, 2004), p.6.

Chapter 14: Pray for the Living and the Dead
1. G.K. Chesterton, *The Everlasting Man* (San Francisco: Ignatius, 1993), pp. 187–188.
2. See "Apocatastasis" in the *Catholic Encyclopedia*, www.new advent.org.
3. Hugh Hewitt, "A Conversation with Christopher Hitchens," July 14, 2010, www.hughhewitt.com/blog.

Alexander, Matthew and John Bruning. *How to Break a Terrorist: The U.S. Interrogators Who Used Brains, Not Brutality, to Take Down the Deadliest Man in Iraq.* New York: Free Press, 2008.

Aquinas, Thomas. *Summa Theologiae.* Available online at www.newadvent.org/summa/.

Athanasius. *On the Incarnation.* Yonkers, N.Y.: St. Vladimir's Seminary Press, 1996.

Chesterton, G.K. *The Everlasting Man.* San Francisco: Ignatius, 1993.

———. *Heretics.* New York: John Lane, 1905.

Lewis, C.S. *The Complete C.S. Lewis: Signature Classics.* New York: HarperCollins, 2002.

———. *The Great Divorce.* New York: HarperCollins, 2000.

———. *The Magician's Nephew.* New York: HarperCollins, 1998.

———. *The Screwtape Letters.* New York: HarperCollins, 2001.

Hugo, Victor. *Les Miserables.* New York: Signet Classics, 1987.

Newman, John Henry. *Apologia Pro Vita Sua.* London: Longman, 1878.

O'Driscoll, Mary. *Catherine of Siena: Passion for the Truth—Compassion for Humanity.* Hyde Park, N.Y.: New City, 2005.

Tolkien, J.R.R. *The Lord of the Rings.* New York: Random House, 2001.